CONTENTS

Introduction   4

1 ——— **History: Before the Revolution**   5
First Encounters   *5*
¡Viva Cuba Libre!   *8*
From Moncada to Revolution   *12*

2 ——— **History of the Revolution: Island in the Storm**   14
Daggers Drawn   *15*
The Communist Cause   *16*
To Market   *20*
The Cost of Change   *24*

3 ——— **Politics: Party and People**   26
Mass Organizations   *27*
The Security Apparatus   *29*
U.S.-Cuban Relations   *31*
Whither Cuba?   *37*

4 ——— **Economy: State and Market**   40
A Tale of Two Superpowers   *40*
Parallel Economies   *43*
Tourism   *47*
Economic Outlook   *49*

5 ——— **Society: Diversity and Equality**   51
Ethnic Mix   *51*
Religion   *53*
Women   *57*
Education   *58*

6 ——— **Culture: Caribbean Fusion**   64
Music   *69*
Film   *72*
Literature   *74*
Sport   *75*

Conclusion   78

Where to Go, What to See   80
Tips for Travelers   85
Addresses and Contacts   88
Further Reading   89
Facts and Figures   90

INTRODUCTION

With its 25 floors and lavish use of concrete, the Hilton Hotel must have seemed the height of fashion when it opened in the 1950s. Like many other hotels in the Vedado district of Havana, the Hilton represented the power of the American Mafia and the dictator Batista, who between them controlled the city at the time. It was no accident that when Fidel Castro and his band of revolutionaries triumphed in January 1959, they chose a hotel as their headquarters. They renamed the Hilton the *Habana Libre* ("Free Havana"). Awash with young rebels in their fatigues, it became the symbol of Cuba's hope for a better future. The doors of the Hilton were opened to Cubans of any class or color. Cuba had been reclaimed for the people.

The American Buicks and Chevrolets that cruised the streets in the 1950s still splutter along the streets of Havana, past buildings that have hardly been touched since before Castro entered the city. In a typically Cuban anomaly, while time has seemingly stood still, life has also changed dramatically.

Fidel Castro put Cuba on the world map. He provided healthcare and education on a scale that his people had not dared to dream about. He helped to shake up a society rigidly segregated along class and racial lines. He was an inspiration to oppressed peoples and to socialists around the world.

The advances that have elevated the island above its partners in the developing world, have also raised Cubans' expectations and given them ambitions that their government can no longer satisfy. The economic crisis that struck the island following the collapse of communism in Europe has presented the Revolution with its greatest challenge yet. After almost 40 years under the same leader, the country is grappling with the problem of adapting to a new and often harsh reality.

Now, the country's future is even harder to predict than it was in 1959. Despite the short-term uncertainties, however, compared with most Third World countries the prospects for Cuba's long-term future are good. Economically, the Caribbean's largest and most fertile island has great potential to be prosperous and stable. Furthermore, it has a huge North American market on its doorstep; whether Cuba wishes it or not, the U.S. will almost certainly have as big an influence on its future growth as it has had on its economic decline.

Cuba has no parallel within the developing or the developed world, whether politically, economically, or culturally. The Cuban national identity, a blend of chiefly Spanish and African influences mixed in a turbulent history of nationalism and revolution, is unique. This small country arouses extreme and polarized emotions, but never indifference. For most people who know Cuba, it is nothing less than an addiction.

IN FOCUS

CUBA

A Guide to the People, Politics and Culture

Emily Hatchwell and Simon Calder

LATIN AMERICA BUREAU

INTERLINK BOOKS
NEW YORK

In the U.S.:

Interlink Books
An imprint of Interlink Publishing Group, Inc.
99 Seventh Avenue, Brooklyn, New York 11215

Library of Congress Cataloging-in-Publication Data

Hatchwell, Emily.
Cuba in focus: a guide to the people, politics and culture /
Emily Hatchwell and Simon Calder
p. cm. (In focus)
Includes bibliographical references.
ISBN: 1-56656-241-4 (paperback)
1. Cuba - Description and travel 2. Cuba - Guidebooks.
I. Calder, Simon. II. Title. III. Series: In focus (London,
England)
F1765.3.H38   1999
917.29104'64--dc21   98-27666
                                             CIP

In the U.K.:

Latin America Bureau (Research and Action) Ltd,
1 Amwell Street, London EC1R 1UL

The Latin America Bureau is an independent research and publishing organization. It works to broaden public understanding of issues of human rights and social and economic justice in Latin America and the Caribbean.

A CIP catalogue record for this book is available from the British Library
ISBN: 1 899365 26 5

Editing: James Ferguson
Cover photograph: Simon Calder
Cover design: Andy Dark
Design: Liz Morrell
Cartography and diagrams: Catherine Pyke

Already published in the *In Focus* series:
Argentina, Bolivia, Brazil, Chile, Colombia, Costa Rica, Dominican Republic, Eastern Caribbean, Ecuador, Guatemala, Jamaica, Mexico, Peru, Venezuela

Printed and bound in Hong Kong

1   HISTORY: BEFORE THE REVOLUTION

"One of the most rich and desirable possessions existing in the world"
— General Leonard Wood, 1901

Cubans sometimes refer to their homeland as the "sleeping alligator" because of its shape. This imaginary creature lies at the western end of the Antilles chain of Caribbean islands, close to the jaws of the Gulf of Mexico. Haiti is just 60 miles east and Key West, the southernmost point of the continental United States, 90 miles to the north. Cuba occupies about the same area as England but stretches over 745 miles from end to end. The capital, Havana, where more than two million of the island's population of eleven million live, sits on the northwestern coast, near where the alligator's tail meets its body.

The island is largely low-lying, with great swathes of central Cuba given over to sugar and citrus plantations. Europeans cross the Atlantic Ocean in order to lie on Cuba's beaches for two weeks, but the country's greatest natural assets are its mountains. There are three main ranges — the Cordillera de Guaniguanico in the west, the central Escambray mountains, and the more rugged Sierra Maestra, which extends along the southeastern coast and sheltered Fidel Castro and his fellow rebels during their guerrilla campaign in the 1950s.

Thousands of islands pepper the waters around Cuba. Most of these show up merely as pinpricks on a map, but the largest encompasses an area of about 890 square miles: this is the Isla de la Juventud or Island of Youth. Once known as the Isla del Tesoro ("Treasure Island") — the inspiration for the title of Robert Louis Stevenson's famous tale of adventure — and the Isla de los Pinos ("Isle of Pines"), the island was given its new name in 1978 in recognition of the thousands of foreign students working and studying there.

First Encounters

Archaeology provides scant rewards in Cuba. The piecing together of the island's early history relies much more on conjecture than on concrete evidence.

Tribes from Central or South America arrived in waves from around 1000BC, possibly even earlier. The Siboneys settled first, making their homes in caves and living off fishing. They survived only in the west of the island at the time of the Conquest, having been forced into a corner by the fiercer Taínos, a tribe of Arawak Indians who came from the Orinoco basin on the South American mainland — some as late as 1460. The Taínos farmed and made ceramic pots, activities that represented the peak of sophistication in pre-Columbian Cuba. They enslaved the less-advanced Siboneys but were a peaceable tribe, ill-disposed to take much of a stand against the European *conquistadores*.

Christopher Columbus caught his first glimpse of Cuba on October 27, 1492 and declared that he had "never seen anything so beautiful." Convinced that he had reached the Asian continent of the Great Khan, he sent his men off in search of "a king and great cities." They found only small villages of thatched huts — the so-called *bohíos*, which still pepper the Cuban countryside — and people inhaling the smoke of "certain herbs": this was the Europeans' first encounter with tobacco, one of the few legacies left by the Indians.

The Takeover

Spain showed little interest in Cuba at first. Occupation by the Europeans began finally in 1511, when Diego Velásquez disembarked with 300 men near Guantánamo Bay in the southeast. It was a swift and cruel affair which was wrapped up by 1514. The only real resistance was led by Hatuey, a fearsome Indian from the neighboring island of Hispaniola, who tried to rally the Taínos by recounting tales of the Spanish atrocities from which he and others had fled. His reception was lukewarm, however, and he was eventually caught. Hatuey preferred death by fire to conversion to the Christianity of his captors.

The early *conquistadores* came merely in search of easy spoils, and as soon as Cuba's gold ran out many of them headed off to the richer pastures of Mexico and Peru. Only geography prevented complete neglect of the island. Placed neatly at the mouth of the Gulf of Mexico, Cuba was crucial in protecting Spanish ships traveling between the New World colonies and Europe against attack by foreign fleets and pirates. The fledgling capital of Havana soon boasted Latin America's most formidable collection of fortresses and became the assembly point for Spanish ships heading back across the Atlantic.

Away from the hubbub of maritime activity in Havana, development was haphazard. The *encomienda* system, which gave the first colonizers a piece of land and a certain number of Indians to work it, was a feudal system infinitely worse than anything that existed in Spain. It forced the indigenous people into a life of slavery which in the end destroyed them; those who did not die of malnutrition, disease, or maltreatment, killed themselves.

Slaves were shipped in from Africa to replace the depleted workforce. Many ended up on sugar plantations, where they were obliged to live like animals in huts called *barracones*. Slave-owners forced the strongest, healthiest men to breed with the fittest women to produce children whom they could then sell for a good price at auction. Rebellious slaves, known as *cimarrones*, fled their infernal lives and formed communities called *palenques*, mostly in the mountainous Oriente. A few lucky Africans were able to buy their liberty, while others were released by masters undergoing deathbed repentances.

Distinctive landscape of Viñales Valley, with tobacco crop

(Rolando Pujol/South American Pictures)

A Case of Monopoly

The island's economy made only slow progress during the early colonial period, and until the eighteenth century Cuba's claim to be "The Pearl of the Antilles" was largely wishful thinking. It was foreign intervention that finally woke Cuba from its torpor.

Spain had faced competition from other European powers in the Caribbean for some time, and in 1762 the British finally managed to capture Havana. They returned the city to Spain in exchange for Florida after just eleven months, but during their short stay managed to change the course of Cuban history. By dropping the trade restrictions that had banned the island from doing business with any country other than Spain, the British opened up a new market for their merchants and helped to launch Cuba's export trade.

Back in Spanish hands, Cuba's economy received another unexpected boost in 1791, when a slave uprising in the French-ruled half of Hispaniola, now Haiti, destroyed that territory's sugar industry. Almost overnight, Cuba took over the role as the largest producer of sugar in the Caribbean. The island's hardwood forests and grazing lands disappeared beneath a blanket of sugar-cane. In 1818, a royal decree opened Cuban ports to international trade and fueled the sugar boom further.

The speed of economic development was matched by growing frustration among the creoles (*criollos*), people of Spanish descent born on the island. Some of them had achieved considerable success as cattle-breeders and tobacco and sugar planters, but found their horizons curtailed by Spanish rule. The so-called *peninsulares*, born in Spain, formed an elite that not only controlled trade but was guaranteed the administration's top jobs, leaving the *criollos* with no say in the running of the country. The economic struggle gradually turned into a battle for political power, and ultimately for sovereignty.

¡Viva Cuba Libre!

Many of the wealthiest *criollo* bourgeoisie favored reform, but not necessarily a revolution. Greater than their desire for independence was their fear of the Afro-Cubans — a sentiment they shared with the *peninsulares* and one that developed into hysteria following the revolt in Haiti and the rapid rise in the number of slaves that accompanied Cuba's sugar boom; by the 1840s, slaves made up as much as 45 percent of the population. Such fears were deep-seated enough to delay Cuba's bid for independence until well after other Latin American countries (except Puerto Rico) had liberated themselves from Spain. Gradually, the impetus for independence passed to the *criollos* of Oriente. Left behind by the sugar boom in the west, small planters in Cuba's eastern province had little to lose by upsetting the status quo. One such plantation owner called Carlos Manuel de Céspedes launched Cuba's first war of liberation on October 10, 1868 by freeing his slaves.

Máximo Gómez, a defector from the Spanish army, and Antonio Maceo, a bold mulatto known as the "Titan of Bronze," led a spirited military campaign. They were eventually defeated not on the battlefield but by their *criollo* backers, who could not overcome their mistrust of the peasants and ex-slaves who made up the rebel army, and capitulated to the Spanish in 1878. The Ten Years' War had killed more than 250,000 Cubans, including Céspedes, shattered illusions and destroyed the sugar industry. Nevertheless, it contributed to the abolition of slavery in 1886 and laid the ground for the next confrontation.

José Martí

A short man with a long, melancholy mustache, José Martí was an unlikely leader of Cuba's independence struggle. Exiled to Spain in 1870 for his separatist views, he made his way to the United States, where he wrote tirelessly and traveled around Cuban émigré communities to unite a revolutionary movement demoralized by defeat. Martí was the first man to define exactly what the independence movement should be fighting for: not just self-rule but democracy and social justice. He advocated racial equality and rallied behind him both Afro-Cubans, who had escaped slavery but not misery, and mixed-race Cubans who faced systematic discrimination. They were joined by an increasingly class-conscious urban workforce and growing ranks of the frustrated middle class.

Martí believed that the Ten Years' War had been lost through bad organization. He founded the Cuban Revolutionary Party (PRC), to unify all those behind independence, and persuaded Maceo and Gómez to plan the new military strategy. The campaign began near Santiago in the east of the island on February 24, 1895. Facing a force five times its size, the liberation army pushed the enemy steadily westwards until by 1898, Spain and its commanders were exhausted both militarily and economically. With the Cubans on the brink of triumph, the U.S. snatched victory.

How the War Was Won

José Martí, shot dead in battle on May 19, 1895, had warned of North American expansionism. In a letter to a friend he had written, "Once the United States is in Cuba, who will get it out?" The Americans had long coveted the island, and as early as 1807, Thomas Jefferson commented that Cuba would make a valuable addition to the United States. With an eye to a business opportunity, Americans had eagerly pursued Cuban planters left impoverished after the Ten Years' War and bought up property at bargain prices. They soon dominated the sugar industry, and by 1895 more than 90 percent of Cuba's sugar went to the U.S., along with the vast majority of its other exports.

Washington was reluctant to sacrifice such a profitable relationship for the sake of Cuban independence. Following the sinking in Havana harbor of an American ship, the *USS Maine*, in February 1898, Washington accused the Spanish of sabotage and declared war. (It was never proved that Spain was to blame, and the evidence points the finger at the Americans themselves.) Within months the colonial army surrendered to an American occupying force. The Treaty of Paris, signed on December 10, 1898, was negotiated behind the backs of the islanders and transferred sovereignty of Cuba to the United States.

Washington contemplated annexation but in the end allowed the Cubans to elect their own government. There was much jubilation on May 20, 1902, as Cuba was declared a Republic, acquired its first president, in the shape of Tomás Estrada Palma, and American troops began to withdraw. But the price paid for the end of military occupation was the acceptance of the Platt Amendment, which proclaimed Washington's right to intervene at any time "for the preservation of Cuban independence." It also provided for the establishment of the U.S. naval station at Guantánamo Bay, 50 miles east of Santiago, to be leased "in perpetuity." The Amendment was repealed in 1934, but the naval base remained and has been a continual source of aggravation for Fidel Castro's government.

The Years of the Fat Cows

More than 300,000 people had died simply to replace rule by Spain with economic and political control by the U.S. Fidel Castro in his speeches still

Cuban independence fighters face Spanish imperial troops in 1898 (Mary Evans Picture Library)

refers to the five decades which followed independence as the "pseudo" or "neo-colonial" republic. American monopolies cornered almost every sphere of activity. By 1925, they controlled electricity generation and owned the railways, while the Cuban Telephone Company did not even bother to give its network a Spanish name. However, it was sugar that held the key to U.S. domination. By the 1920s, U.S. companies produced more than half the annual crop. Small farmers were squeezed out by the large estates created to meet their northern neighbor's appetite for sugar. Other crops and industry were neglected, forcing Cuba to import everything from tomatoes to cars, supplied (most conveniently) by the U.S. Business bank accounts swelled while ordinary Cubans endured increasing poverty. Amid rising anger at the corruption of politicians, Gerardo Machado won the presidency in 1924 with his slogan "honesty in government." He started out reasonably well but later introduced Cuba to its first brutal military dictatorship.

Social unrest intensified steadily until the labor movement, galvanized by the Communist Party, called a general strike in 1933. The show of popular discontent succeeded in toppling Machado and sparked a mini-revolution by an unlikely alliance of militant students from Havana University — a traditional hotbed of radical thought — and dissatisfied sergeants under a certain Fulgencio Batista. The army, however, had no intention of collaborating with the reformist government that emerged, and after three months Batista (by then a colonel) staged a coup.

The Rise of Batista

Batista enjoyed some initial popularity. A handsome mulatto of lower-class origins, he was a rarity among Cuba's ruling oligarchy, which was traditionally rich and white. While he manipulated a string of elections and presidents, he also helped to implement one of the most progressive constitutions in Latin America. He also legalized the trade unions and even introduced welfare reform. Batista's flirtation with the Communist Party helped him to win the presidential elections in 1940, but he could not repeat the trick in 1944. He went into "voluntary exile" while first Ramón Grau and then Carlos Prío were voted into the top job.

The Cuban people, disgusted by political corruption, oppression, and their continued poverty, had begun rallying around Eduardo Chibás, leader of the Orthodox Party. His calls for social justice made him a contender in the elections of 1952, but suffering from severe depression, Chibás shocked Cuba by shooting himself during a live radio broadcast on August 5, 1951. With his last words "People of Cuba, rise and move forward! People of Cuba, awake!" etched in their memory, Cubans watched in horror as Batista returned from exile and, on March 10, 1952, staged a coup.

Fulgencio Batista imposed the harshest dictatorship Cuba had yet seen. He abolished the Constitution, dissolved Congress, and crushed the opposition ruthlessly. Thousands died in the violence, but that did not deter support from Washington.

Cuba enjoyed one of the highest per capita incomes in Latin America but wavered on the edge of social collapse. Misery reigned in the countryside while Havana glittered. The Cuban capital was one of Latin America's most sophisticated cities, and a byword for hedonism the world over.

The "Fabulous Fifties"

Havana was one of the most fashionable places in the world. A pantheon of America's rich and famous, from Marilyn Monroe to Errol Flynn, arrived by plane or ferry from Florida. They glided around the Cuban capital in Cadillacs, which still cruise the streets today, and entertained themselves drinking *daiquiris* and *mojitos* at Sloppy Joe's or the Floridita, Ernest Hemingway's favorite haunt. They splashed their money about the casinos, or sought titillation from the sex shows at the Shanghai Theatre or from Havana's answer to the Folies Bergères, the Tropicana. Frank Sinatra was reputedly paid $1,000 a night to perform at this, Latin America's most extravagant variety show. Graham Greene took Mr. Wormold to it in *Our Man in Havana*: "Chorus-girls paraded twenty feet up among the great palm-trees, while pink and mauve searchlights swept the floor. A man in bright blue evening clothes sang in Anglo-American about Paree."

The Mafia swooped down on Havana with ambitious plans to turn it into an offshore Las Vegas. Fulgencio Batista and the gangsters controlled tourism between them, and they built many of the high-rise hotels which still fill the skyline of Havana's Vedado district. Meyer Lansky, who had had associations with Cuba ever since the 1920s (when he used the island as a supply base for rum sold in the Prohibition-stricken U.S.), was Havana's chief mobster. A hundred representatives of the Cosa Nostra, as well as celebrities such as Ginger Rogers and Lou Costello, attended the opening in December 1957 of the luxurious Habana Riviera Hotel, whose casino became Lansky's headquarters. When the Revolution forced Batista to flee, the Mafia went too. Their roulette and fruit machines were thrown out onto the street, and gambling in all its forms remains illegal to this day.

From Moncada to Revolution

On July 26, 1953, a young lawyer named Fidel Castro and 125 other militants attacked the Moncada barracks in Santiago de Cuba. The assault was as disastrous as it was daring, leaving most of the assailants dead. However, the 26-year-old ringleader survived to stand trial and give the first great speech of his life. The speech, in which he set out a program for the regeneration of the island, became the basis for the political vision of Cuba's new revolutionary front, the 26 of July Movement — named after the now sacred date of the Moncada assault and dedicated to armed insurrection.

Despite a sentence of fifteen years in prison, popular pressure forced Batista to grant Fidel Castro and his fellow rebels an amnesty in May 1955. Forbidden from making public speeches, Castro left for Mexico City. A group of idealistic young revolutionaries gathered around him there, including his brother Raúl and a young Argentinian doctor called Ernesto "Che" Guevara.

"It wasn't a disembarkation, it was a shipwreck" was Guevara's description of the landing of *Granma*, a leaking six-berth cabin cruiser which brought Castro and 81 revolutionaries from Mexico to Cuba in December 1956. The rebels lost almost all their equipment, and only thirteen men — including Fidel, Raúl, and Che — made it to Pico Turquino in the Sierra Maestra mountains west of Santiago.

From such small beginnings, an extraordinary insurgency developed. The rebels spent the first six months winning over the peasants, whose collaboration Castro knew was vital to the cause. Promises of agrarian reform inspired several thousand of the largely landless farmers and laborers to join the ranks of the Rebel Army. Fidel Castro and his men were in control of the Sierra Maestra within a year.

A military stalemate ensued, with the rebels unable to break out of the mountains, and Batista's army of 50,000 unable to defeat the guerrillas on their own territory. In the end, it was agitation in the cities by the 26 of July Movement and other groups which drove Batista to make a move. In mid-1958 he launched his biggest attack ever against the rebels. It was a fiasco, and Castro responded by launching a counter-offensive in August, sending two columns westwards towards Havana. An attack by Che Guevara's column on a government troop train in Santa Clara in December 1958 was a defining moment in the downfall of the dictatorship.

With his armed forces rebellious, Batista fled to the Dominican Republic on January 1, 1959. A general strike called immediately afterwards showed overwhelming support for the rebels and the army surrendered. Fidel Castro made a triumphal procession across the island from Santiago, greeted along the way by thousands of ecstatic Cubans. He arrived in the capital on January 8, but a more memorable date, New Year's Day, marks the anniversary of the Revolution's triumph — Liberation Day.

Fidel Castro, Raúl Castro and Che Guevara, 1959 (Osvaldo Salas/Reportage)

Fidel Castro

Fidel Castro Ruz, born in 1927 in Holguín province, was the second of five illegitimate children born to a Galician plantation owner and his cook. His upbringing was strictly bourgeois; he attended a Catholic and then a Jesuit school, and in 1945 entered Havana University. Castro graduated in law in 1951, but politics was the young man's passion. He tried conventional politics and joined the Orthodox Party, but after Batista's coup he concluded that armed insurrection was the only option.

Fidel Castro's success as a revolutionary leader has been due partly to his astonishing intellect — he has a remarkable ability to absorb information about anything from the latest women's fashions to sewage treatment — but also to his determination, charisma, and ability to win affection: few citizens of the world are on first name terms, as are Cubans, with their leader. His personal influence has been decisive in guiding the people through the vicissitudes of the last 40 years.

Despite the sobriquet, *El Jefe Máximo* ("The Maximum Leader"), Castro has never encouraged a Stalinist cult of personality. His portrait adorns many an office wall and his speeches are published verbatim in the newspapers, but you will see no statues of him, no streets named after him. The image and name of José Martí appear on far more billboards than do those of Fidel Castro.

Cubans have an enormous capacity to talk, but none more than Fidel Castro. He can speak for hours without a break and without the aid of notes. His record is fourteen hours, although that was many years ago. While he still has an awesome ability to arouse a crowd, his speeches have grown considerably shorter and he has certainly lost some of the electric rhetoric of his youth. He has also grown noticeably leaner and his famous beard is grey and thinning.

Fidel Castro envelops himself in a thick cocoon of protection and secrecy. The silence imposed on the media, which is forbidden to publish or report anything about the Cuban leader's personal life, inevitably breeds rumors. All kinds of stories circulate about his relationships with women and his illegitimate offspring. Officially he has two children, Fidelito and Alina, both of whom now live abroad. Alina, who escaped to the U.S. in 1993 disguised as a Spanish tourist, is one of the few sources of details about Fidel's private life. According to her memoirs, her father writes romantic poetry and finds his trademark fatigues uncomfortable.

Having divorced his wife, Mirta Díaz Balart, in 1955, Fidel Castro has never remarried. Celia Sánchez, his assistant in the Sierra Maestra and later in Havana, was the closest companion Fidel Castro ever had. Since her death of cancer in 1980, the Cuban leader has cut a rather lonely figure.

2 HISTORY OF THE REVOLUTION: ISLAND IN THE STORM

"History will absolve me"
— Fidel Castro, 1953

Euphoria swept through Cuba in January 1959. The daring young revolutionaries became folk heroes overnight. Banners around Havana read "Power to the Bearded Ones" (a reference to the abundant facial hair sported by many rebels on their descent from the mountains). Yet amid all the excitement Cubans began to wonder what lay in store. Firstly, the band of young rebels had absolutely no experience of running a country. Secondly, from the mountains Fidel Castro had promised something to everyone — from agrarian reform to political democracy. Havana's white bourgeoisie was unsure what to make of the white, middle class-turned-peasant soldiers whose approach to discipline verged on the puritanical. Some took fright and fled the island. Others seemed to think there would be a few reforms, free elections, and then a return to business as usual. It soon became clear, however, that Cuba was in for radical change.

But first there was retribution, for the murder of as many as 20,000 Cubans during the repressive campaigns of the 1950s. Calls for revenge rang louder than those for legal formality. Revolutionary Tribunals, set up to deal with the so-called *Batistianos*, presided over show trials which sent most of the accused to the firing squad.

Taking Control

Soon after the *triunfo* (triumph), Fidel Castro and his rebels appointed Manuel Urrutia (a judge who had been sympathetic to their cause) as president, to head a government made up of representatives of the old political parties. But conflict quickly developed between the presidential palace and the Habana Libre Hotel, formerly the Hilton, where Castro and his men were lodged in the early days, and where real authority lay. Urrutia was replaced by Osvaldo Dórticos, a more obedient figurehead president, while the old moderates in government were gently eased out in favor of *Fidelistas*.

The government passed more than 1,500 laws in its first year. Measures included pay increases and radically reduced rents. Most dramatically, the Agrarian Reform Act decreed that any farm with more than 1,000 acres of land would pass to the state. Within a year the government had acquired more than 40 percent of Cuba's hitherto foreign-dominated farmland. Some of this was redistributed to landless peasants, but much of it was reorganized into state farms, providing secure jobs for laborers who had long suffered the so-called "dead time" between harvests.

Many of the early reforms put money in the pockets of the poor over-night and won the government immediate popularity, but that did not stop speculation about elections. Castro, who had promised free elections from the Sierra Maestra, now stated that "the Revolution has no time to waste in such foolishness." The regime claimed that people showed their support by attending rallies, in a process it dubbed "direct democracy." The government's confidence was not misplaced, given its popularity at the time, but its suspension of the constitution and refusal to seek a popular mandate provided extra ammunition for outside observers, above all in the U.S., whose government was increasingly alarmed at developments on the island.

The United States had maintained a fickle position during the war, initially supplying Batista with arms, later asking him to stand down and eventually recognizing the new regime in Havana. Within months, however, it became apparent that Cuba and its powerful neighbor were destined for confrontation.

Daggers Drawn

Agrarian reform ruffled plenty of feathers in the U.S., but it was wholesale nationalization which put an end to any chance of peaceful coexistence. During 1960, the Cuban government expropriated all American assets from oil refineries to the telephone network. By the end of the year there was almost nothing left that did not belong to the state. In a series of tit-for-tat measures, the Americans responded by reducing the quota of sugar it bought from Cuba, and then, in October 1960, by canceling sugar purchases completely and prohibiting all exports to Cuba except of food and medical supplies. President Eisenhower broke off diplomatic relations in January 1961, and soon afterwards the new man in the White House, John F. Kennedy, gave the go-ahead for an invasion, to be led by U.S.-based exiles.

The Bay of Pigs

Political considerations aside, the Bay of Pigs attack was a shambles from its very inception. The idea that the people of Cuba would rise up against Castro following an invasion showed a complete lack of understanding of the situation on the island. Furthermore, everyone knew that the Cuban exiles had been under CIA training from as early as March 1960. Cuba was armed to the hilt by the time the invasion finally happened, with a huge militia force ready to defend the country.

American bombers failed utterly to destroy the Cuban airforce in advance of the land attack on April 17, 1961. This left Castro's pilots free to bomb U.S. navy vessels waiting offshore, while an army of rebels and peasants dealt briskly with the enemy on the ground. The whole operation was defeated within just 48 hours. Just over 1,200 of the 1,500 exiles were captured and eventually exchanged for $53 million worth of supplies from the United States.

While Kennedy had been humiliated, Castro was jubilant. David had beaten Goliath in what the Cuban leader called the "first defeat of U.S. imperialism in the Americas." The incident gave a great boost to the Cubans and Fidel Castro's popularity rocketed. Meanwhile, Kennedy became obsessed with trying to topple the Cuban leader and started sponsoring all kinds of crazy projects. The CIA sent thousands of agents on missions to do just that, and set up its largest station on the campus of the University of Miami. When direct sabotage and the provision of aid to insurgents on the island failed to bring the regime down, the CIA concentrated on ridiculous attempts to assassinate the Cuban leader, using everything from exploding cigars to cyanide capsules.

The Communist Cause

On April 16, 1961, the day after U.S. planes bombed Cuban airfields in the prelude to the Bay of Pigs attack, Castro declared: "They can't forgive our being right here under their noses, seeing how we have made a revolution, a socialist revolution right here under the very noses of the United States!" Two months later, communists from the pre-Castro Communist Party were included in the ruling political alliance, from which the *Partido Comunista de Cuba* or Cuban Communist Party was to spring in 1965. Amid universal speculation as to the political hue of the Cuban regime, news of Castro's shift towards communism reverberated around the world.

Fidel Castro had done nothing either before or after the triumph of the Revolution to dispel the mystery surrounding his ideological leanings. But on December 2, 1961, at the end of a tumultuous year, he explained to the nation, "I am a Marxist-Leninist, and I shall be to the day I die." Later, Castro said that he had hidden the fact that he was a Marxist in order to generate broader support for his revolution. But some Cuba-watchers view his emergence as a communist as evidence more of arch-pragmatism than political conviction, suggesting that it was part of his bid to prove his Marxist credentials to Moscow. With Cuba facing complete isolation by the U.S., Cuba had no option but to find a new protector. The situation was simple: without Soviet support the Revolution would not survive.

Posters proclaiming "Cuba is not alone" appeared in Havana. Moscow had its doubts, however, about supporting a revolution that was neither inspired nor imposed by the USSR. Furthermore, Cuba was on the other side of the world and not easy to control. Yet, in the end, the prospect of having a client state in the Caribbean was irresistible. Hence, when the Cubans suddenly found themselves bereft of their American market, the USSR bailed them out. A delegation from Moscow agreed in February 1960 to an oil-for-sugar swap, which helped sustain the Cuban economy through to the late 1980s. Trade with the other socialist countries also expanded rapidly. In

Revolutionary volunteer and peasant during
literacy campaign of early 1960s

(Osvaldo Salas/Reportage)

1959, Eastern Europe had been the destination for 2.2 percent of Cuba's exports; by 1962, this was 82 percent. Imports from the Eastern bloc rose from 0.3 percent to 70 percent.

The Russo-Cuban alliance was a curious friendship. Cuba had far more in common with its enemy, North America, than with its new ally, the USSR. For its part, the Kremlin could not resist maximizing political advantage from its new strategic position in the United States' "backyard."

The Missile Crisis

Premier Khrushchev's statement in July 1960, that the USSR would defend Cuba against an American attack with its own missiles, owed as much to bravado as to genuine enthusiasm for its role as protector. Yet when Castro requested military aid in 1962, amid fears that the United States was contemplating a full-scale invasion of the island, Moscow seized the opportunity to locate nuclear missiles within reach of its Cold War enemy. (There is evidence that preparations were indeed underway in the U.S. for such a war.)

More than 40 nuclear missiles had arrived in Cuba by the time President Kennedy got wind of it. He was outraged that the USSR was threatening the balance of power in the region. On October 22, 1962, Kennedy announced that the U.S. navy would stop any Russian ships on the way to Cuba carrying offensive weapons. He demanded the withdrawal of missiles already on the

Cuban exiles captured during abortive
Bay of Pigs invasion, April 1961
(Hulton Deutsch)

island, and declared that the United States would not shrink from nuclear war if it came to that. Khrushchev refused to cooperate. For six days the Soviet convoy continued towards Cuba and the awaiting American ships, while in the U.S. nuclear weapons were prepared for launching. The world held its breath until Khrushchev finally backed down, proposing that the Russians would withdraw their weapons if the U.S. pledged not to invade Cuba. Kennedy agreed. The two superpowers had been teetering on the brink of nuclear war.

With the conclusion of the Cuban Missile Crisis, the stage was set for the duel which has persisted ever since. President Kennedy tightened up the trade embargo and promised, "We will build a wall around Cuba." The American president was not destined to see the results of this policy, however, since he was assassinated the following year. Suspicions continue among some in the U.S. that Kennedy was killed by Cuban exiles, who were frustrated that the President did not deal more aggressively with Castro.

Domestic Opposition

Immediately after the rebels' triumph, the counter-revolutionary effort within Cuba consisted mainly of sabotage attacks against industrial installations and sugar mills, plus a small-scale insurgency in the Escambray mountains; both activities were largely made possible thanks to help from the CIA. The small army of *bandidos* was defeated as a serious force by the end of 1960, but it took until 1966 for the Rebel Army to flush out the last of the counter-revolutionaries. In the end, thousands of guerrillas were killed and local sympathizers were forced from their homes.

One reason that the Revolution succeeded in establishing itself comparatively easily was the emigration of half a million of the most disgruntled Cubans by the end of the 1960s. The majority were members of the urban white middle class, who settled mainly in Miami. With much of the impetus for counter-revolution based abroad, a sustained challenge from within Cuba became impossible.

There was also repression. Anyone who was not with the Revolution was by definition against it. Trade unions were disbanded and the media came under direct government control. Neighborhood Committees for the Defense of the Revolution, or CDRs, were founded early on to help prevent counter-revolutionary activity: members would report the suspicious behavior of neighbors to the authorities. By 1965, an estimated 60,000 political prisoners were in Cuban jails and work camps.

The Military Units for Aid to Production (UMAP) represent one of the darkest moments of the Revolution. These labor camps were set up by the army in 1965 for the ideological rehabilitation of "social deviants," a loose term which embraced anyone who was perceived as a threat to the Revolution, particularly homosexuals, dissident intellectuals, and also Catholics. Relgious beliefs were considered to be anti-revolutionary.

The Revolution in Progress

With immediate threats to the Revolution contained, greater attention could be directed towards social and economic development.

In the early years of the Revolution, vast amounts of money were invested in the provision of healthcare, education, and housing. One of the most famous government campaigns of the 1960s was its literacy campaign, in which around 250,000 young volunteers were dispatched into the countryside to teach the Cubans neglected by pre-revolutionary regimes to read and write. Numerous schools and universities were built. In the field of healthcare, clinics sprang up all over the country, the number of doctors rocketed, and infant mortality rates were slashed.

As Minister of Industry and President of the National Bank, Che Guevara oversaw the Cuban economy for five years: this was the most radical phase of the Revolution. Despite his inexperience in the field, Guevara dreamed up a program that was designed to overhaul not only the Cuban economy but also society as a whole. Fundamental to his plan for the redistribution of wealth was the rigid centralization of the economy; by 1968, the government had nationalized all Cuba's private businesses, down to the last hot dog stand. The only exclusion was the permitted private farming sector. The market laws of supply and demand were thrown out, as were ideas of profit. Unemployment became a thing of the past.

As controversial as his economic changes was Guevara's idealistic vision of the *Hombre Nuevo* or "New Man," the worker who replaces bourgeois ambitions of personal gain with elevated ideas of collective advancement.

Cubans started working extra hours not for more pay, but for the honor of receiving praise in the local paper or a congratulatory banner: voluntary work for the good of the community. Much of the new housing that appeared all over the island was built by so-called "micro-brigades" of volunteers.

The regime's economic policies, coupled with the effects of the U.S. embargo and the exodus of the country's most skilled professionals, resulted in empty factories and inefficiency. The economy lurched from crisis to crisis. Agricultural production plummeted and rationing was introduced in 1962 (and has remained part of life in Cuba ever since). Guevara resigned in 1965 to go and do what he liked doing best, fighting other people's wars and trying to mobilize a continent-wide revolution in Latin America. Meanwhile, the regime ambitiously tried to mobilize hundreds of thousands of Cubans to reap a bumper 10-million-ton sugar harvest in 1970 — and thereby solve the island's economic woes at a stroke. Not only did the attempt fail, but it also disrupted the whole economy in the process. With its economy in tatters, Cuba headed deeper into the Soviet fold, a step dictated partly by Russian promises of substantial aid if Havana abandoned Guevara's Maoist program in favor of a more orthodox communist line. Self-sufficiency had proved an impossible dream.

The early 1970s were tough and repressive years, but by 1975 the regime felt confident enough to stage the first Communist Party Congress. This launched a whole new political system of national and local government, which was designed to spread decision-making away from Havana. However, in reality, the hegemony of the Party remained untouched by the new assemblies of *Poder Popular* or People's Power. A new constitution, approved by a referendum in 1976, recognized Marxism-Leninism as the state ideology and the Communist Party as the only legal political organization in the country. Fidel Castro's position as head of state became constitutional. Osvaldo Dórticos, puppet president since 1959, retired.

To Market

If the 1975 Party Congress centralized political power, it also began a phase in which the government tried to loosen its grip on the economy, particularly in the field of agriculture. The goal of the communist regime had always been for the state to control the entire agricultural sector, and after the Revolution most sugar plantations had been transformed into vast, Soviet-style state farms. Cooperatives, where workers shared the profits, were also set up, but were dissolved almost immediately because neither Castro nor Guevara was in favor of them. Nevertheless, the private sector still accounted for about 30 percent of agricultural land and proved to be far more productive than the state sector. Accordingly, cooperatives were revitalized after 1976, although the political goal of ultimate state control was not abandoned.

The economy had improved modestly by the end of the decade. Even so, 1980 saw the most serious discontent against the Revolution ever witnessed.

In April of that year, twelve dissidents forced their way into the Peruvian embassy in Havana to seek asylum. More than 10,000 Cubans followed. Probably relishing Castro's discomfort amid such a crisis, President Carter announced that the U.S. would welcome political refugees with "an open heart and open arms." Castro, said to be enraged by the remark, replied by opening the port of Mariel near Havana and permitting an exodus. The number of Cubans wishing to leave may have embarrassed the regime, but always a master at turning a crisis to his advantage, Castro used the boatlift to get rid of several thousand criminals, mental patients, homosexuals, and other "undesirables." It was Carter who eventually called a halt to the five-month flood in which 125,000 Cubans left.

Revolutionaries dubbed the defectors *escoria* or "scum"; they were barely more popular in the U.S. The largely middle-class exile community in Miami disliked the social make-up of the so-called *Marielitos* — most were poor and many were black — on whom they still blame their city's crime problem.

Presumably shocked by such a demonstration of dissatisfaction, Castro immediately sought to improve the quality of life in Cuba. In an attempt to boost food production, he introduced private agricultural markets, where farmers could sell any produce surplus to the quota they supplied to the state. These proved to be such a success that Cubans ate better than they had in years. However, the government became convinced that it had created a class of *nouveau riche* speculators. Having also allowed limited self-employment in some trades, Castro was dismayed, too, by the verve with which Cubans abandoned state jobs in favor of the private sector. In 1986, he implemented the so-called Rectification of Errors, which dissolved the farmers' markets, reinstated hyper-centralization, and put the Party back at the heart of the national economy.

Daily life was a struggle, and rations were reduced. Meanwhile, defense spending rocketed; Ronald Reagan was in the White House and promoting an aggressive policy in the region. In the 1980s, U.S. regional policy led to the invasion of Grenada and sponsorship of the Contra civil war in Nicaragua. At the same time, Rectification was not having the desired effect, but so long as the USSR was willing to shore up the Cuban economy, the regime could weather the worst of the surrounding storms.

Exporting the Revolution

Cuba has been described as a small country with a large country's foreign policy. The island enjoys a surprisingly high profile on the world stage for a country its size. This is largely due to the stance of Fidel Castro's regime against the United States.

After the Revolution, Cuba gave new meaning to the word "internationalism," a mixture of solidarity and pragmatism which became part of the Cuban regime's strategy for survival. Supporting socialist causes abroad was largely an extension of Cuba's own Revolution. Fidel Castro presented Cuba as a model for revolution around the world, and during the 1960s it was indeed an inspiration. He tried to encourage insurrection in Latin America, dreaming of turning the Andes into another Sierra Maestra. In 1966, Che Guevara went to Bolivia in an attempt to foment revolution among the peasants — the first step in his plan to liberate the whole continent. The scheme failed miserably. Guevara was captured by CIA-backed Bolivian troops and killed in October 1967. His body was finally returned to Cuba on the 30th anniversary of his death.

Che Guevara's death marked an end to Cuban interest in Latin America but did not dampen the regime's spirit of internationalism. At times it seemed that every Third World independence or liberation movement had called in the Cubans. Advisors, many doctors and teachers, and sometimes troops were dispatched to numerous countries. Their involvement was greatest in Africa, particularly in Angola, where Havana supported the Marxist government in its struggle against rebels backed by the U.S. and South Africa. More than 370,000 Cubans passed through Angola during the thirteen-year campaign which began in the 1970s, and over 2,000 of them died — mostly through disease. They scored some historic military successes against South Africa, but the 1988 accord was finally reached through negotiation. In exchange for the withdrawal of the 50,000 Cuban troops still in Angola, apartheid South Africa granted Namibia independence in 1990. The campaign in Angola has been dubbed by some as "Cuba's Vietnam," but Fidel Castro's regime has always portrayed it as a great victory against apartheid, an idea supported by Nelson Mandela himself, who sealed his praise of Cuba's contribution to the struggle in South Africa with a visit to the island in 1991.

Even when he was most dependent on subsidies from the USSR, Fidel Castro was a leading light in the Non-Aligned Movement. The invitation to host the 1979 summit of the movement and for Castro to be its president from 1979 to 1982 was a great expression of support for the regime.

The Collapse of European Communism

In the Soviet Union, President Gorbachev had been encouraging reform since the mid-1980s. While the Eastern bloc generally followed suit, Fidel Castro declared that Cuba would sink before it sacrificed socialism; nothing would make the regime deviate from *El Camino Corecto* — "The Right Way." The national media minimized the news of the events taking place in Europe, for fear that the Cubans might rise up against state communism.

The tension in Cuba increased as fast as the power of the Soviet Union decreased. The trial and execution in July 1989 of General Arnaldo Ochoa, a hero of the war in Angola, illustrated an unprecedented degree of nervousness on the part of the regime in Havana. The truth about the Ochoa case may never be known, but at the time the rumors spread that Fidel Castro had the General executed because of his interest in *perestroika* — rather than because of involvement in corruption and drug-trafficking, with which he was charged. Some people even portrayed Ochoa, a charismatic man who was popular among both ordinary Cubans and the soldiers who served under him in Angola, as a potential rival to the leadership.

Ochoa's execution, probably the greatest political scandal in the history of the Revolution, sparked an unprecedented purge of the Ministry of the Interior and was seen as a warning to anyone tempted to undermine the revolution. While Castro was trying to tighten his hold on the nation, across the straits in Miami, right-wing exiles claimed instead that the Cuban leader was losing his grip. Indeed, the odds were stacking up against him. The Berlin Wall had gone and politicians in Moscow mused about the logic of continuing any subsidy to Cuba. The island's fate was sealed in 1992 by the ascent to power of Boris Yeltsin, who was far more concerned about relations with Washington than with Havana. Any historical claim the island had to the USSR's affections became irrelevant once the union ceased to exist.

The Special Period

Since the Soviet bloc accounted for around 85 percent of Cuba's trade, the social and political impact of its collapse was immediate and devastating. Confronted with its biggest economic crisis ever, the government in 1990 implemented the Special Period in Peacetime, an austerity package the likes of which Cubans had never seen.

The most significant shortage was of fuel. Since oil supplies from Eastern Europe (which had met 90 percent of the island's needs) dried up, many factories and offices ceased to function. A large proportion of the Cuban workforce was left with nothing to do but count the *apagones*, the scheduled power cuts that still deprive Cubans of electricity on a regular basis. Public transport ground almost to a halt, leaving people to hitch rides in the back of the few trucks still on the road or to get around by bike; the delivery of thousands of bicycles from China caused the biggest transformation on the streets of Cuba since 1959. Meanwhile, the landscape in the countryside turned medieval, as tractors were replaced by oxen.

The food situation became critical. With fuel for distribution unavailable, crops such as oranges and potatoes were left to rot in the fields, while in towns and cities people stood in ever-growing lines for ever-decreasing rations of a few essentials. In 1989, ration books could more or less guarantee a healthy diet. Within a couple of years this was no longer the case.

The United States, hoping to give the Cuban regime the final nudge over the edge of the precipice, tightened its trade sanctions in 1992. The Cuba Democracy Act, introduced by Congressman Robert Torricelli, brought in a whole variety of restrictive measures, including the extension of the embargo to foreign subsidiaries of U.S. companies. Pleas to exempt food and medical supplies were ignored.

Fidel Castro and Mikhail Gorbachev during
Soviet leader's visit to Cuba, April 1989

(Julio Etchart/Reportage)

The years from 1992–4 were the most critical period of the Revolution. Discontent among Cubans spread, and the number of people trying to reach the U.S. illegally by boat or raft grew steadily. Speculation at home and abroad about the possibility of political and economic reform was rife. The Communist Party Congress of October 1991 had flatly rejected the idea of ideological concessions, asserting that any such change would threaten the Revolution, but delegates did discuss measures to liberalize the economy.

The Cost of Change

It took almost two years for the government to finally implement the first of these liberalizing policies. Article 235 of the Penal Code, which stated that anyone caught in possession of foreign currency could be imprisoned for up to five years, was the first casualty of the regime's reform package. Decriminalizing possession of the dollar (known colloquially as "dollarization") in August 1993 was designed both to harness the dollars circulating in the rampant black economy and to meet some demand for consumer goods unavailable for Cuban pesos in the local shops. Shortly afterwards, the government legalized self-employment in over 100 trades, bringing life to streets empty of small traders since the 1960s.

Dollarization received a mixed reception among Cubans. It was seen as liberating, since for the first time ordinary people could make use of the dollar shops hitherto frequented only by foreign tourists and a few privileged Cubans, but also socially divisive: most people with dollars were anti-Castro, were involved in the black market, or else had relatives in Miami.

Increasingly though, it was Cubans loyal to the party structures who were offered employment in the tourism industry, giving them access to dollars and imported goods. But for the majority of Cubans (including loyal revolutionaries) the goods sold in dollar stores, from essentials such as soap and cooking oil to sandals and jeans, remained the stuff of dreams.

The summer of 1993 saw an unprecedented spate of small demonstrations of discontent in Havana. Castro responded by stepping up vigilance across the island and putting hundreds of suspected troublemakers behind bars. Tension increased steadily until it erupted once more in the summer of 1994. On August 5 of that year, there was a serious riot when police tried to prevent would-be refugees from hijacking a ferry in Havana harbor. Thirty-five police and civilians were injured in the worst unrest since 1959.

Blaming Washington for encouraging Cubans to flee by offering them automatic political asylum in the U.S., Fidel Castro called off the coastguards, inviting an exodus. In a war of nerves, Cuban security forces stood by while refugees set off on boats and makeshift rafts in the hope of being picked up at sea by U.S. coastguard patrols: more than 30,000 were rescued in the space of a month. Within days, President Clinton was forced by domestic political pressures — and the impracticality of handling such a large influx — to reverse the U.S. policy of granting automatic political asylum. U.S. officials moved the boat people or *balseros*, ironically, back to Cuba to be held in camps at the U.S. naval base at Guantánamo. Most were eventually admitted into the U.S.

The following year, the U.S. government conceded that many of those who had left in the exodus had been economic migrants rather than political refugees. An agreement with Cuba was signed, providing for a more orderly outflow of Cubans, with the U.S. agreeing to admit a minimum of 20,000 immigrants a year — compared with a previous average of nearer 3,000. Now, Cubans who leave the island illegally are returned by the American authorities, while Cuba has given the undertaking not to take punitive action against refugees.

The dramatic events of 1994 without doubt helped to speed up the pace of economic reform; private farmers' markets, for instance, were allowed to open soon afterwards. Other reforms followed. Cuba struggled to achieve even limited growth, but confounded any speculation that collapse was only a matter of time.

3   POLITICS: PARTY AND PEOPLE

"To die for your country is to live"
— Cuban National Anthem

Cuban society is the most politicized in the world. The Revolution which provides the people with cradle-to-grave healthcare, also provides cradle-to-grave politics. Cubans grow up well-versed in the achievements of their Revolution and the iniquities of their North American neighbor. Each morning, schools around the country echo with the sound of children chanting "Pioneers for communism, we will be like Che!" The presence of the Revolution and politics in every aspect of daily life in Cuba engenders a bizarre kind of schizophrenia: while at school or in the workplace, Cubans must listen to and utter only good things about the Revolution; at home many will hear or express only disenchantment with the system.

Party Politics

Cuba's daunting array of governing committees and councils, a soup of like-sounding names, conceals the fact that most political power lies in the hands of the Communist Party. Described in the Constitution as "the highest guiding force of society and the State," the Cuban Communist Party (PCC) is the only political party in the country. It is an elite club, made up of the country's top workers and professionals, including those careerists who see Party membership as a vehicle towards the peak of their profession. It penetrates every sphere of activity on the island. No workplace is without its nucleus of Party members, who amount to a national total of some 700,000.

The 150-member Central Committee steers the Communist Party, but an even tighter-knit group, the 24-member *Buró Político* (Politburo), sits at the pinnacle of power. Fidel Castro, as First Secretary, presides over the whole structure. Grassroots members have a chance to discuss policy at meetings in the run-up to each party congress, held every five years, but generally the big policy decisions are decided beforehand by the party leadership.

The assemblies of People's Power (*Poder Popular*), created in 1976, deal with the nuts and bolts of running the country — at provincial and municipal level and through the elected National Assembly, the "supreme organ of state power." The Council of State represents the National Assembly between its twice-yearly sessions and is authorized to issue decrees. Its president (a post invariably belonging to Fidel Castro) is automatically both head of state and head of the government, and also proposes members of the Council of Ministers for approval by the National Assembly. This 44-member council is the highest-ranking executive and administrative organ in the country.

The big names in the Central Committee also dominate the two top government councils.

The National Assembly's close links with the Party (about two-thirds of members belong to the PCC) inevitably lead to accusations that its job is simply to rubber-stamp Communist Party proposals into law. Castro, however, insists that the Cuban political system is "incomparably more democratic than any other," dismissing Western-style democracy as "complete garbage" and Western elections as "beauty contests open to corruption." Since 1993, Cubans have been allowed to elect deputies to the National Assembly in a direct ballot, but they still vote for a single list of candidates: there is just one candidate for each seat in the assembly, who can be rejected only if he or she receives a negative vote of at least 50 percent. The show of obedient hands during voting in the National Assembly illustrates the limits of Cuban "democracy" and the reluctance to gainsay the leadership.

Mass Organizations

The mass organizations cater to the interests of each sector of society, and include the *Central de Trabajadores de Cuba* (CTC), the central trade union organization; the *Federación de Mujeres Cubanas* (FMC), the women's federation; the *Asociación Nacional de Agricultores Pequeños* (ANAP), an association of small private farmers; the *Unión de Jovenes Comunistas* (UJC), the Union of Young Communists; and last but not least the *Comités de Defensa de la Revolución* (CDR), or Committees for the Defense of the Revolution.

The mass organizations are highly politicized, existing as much to rally support for the government as to express their members' particular aspirations. The central trade union organization has a say in decisions on production targets, for example, but unionists were stripped of their right to strike long ago. Nevertheless, the discussions held at grassroots level by these various organizations have become increasingly frank during the Special Period, reflecting the economic and social problems facing many ordinary Cubans.

The Committees for the Defense of the Revolution are the most famous — and notorious — of Cuba's mass organizations. There are said to be more than 100,000 CDRs in Cuba, with a total of over seven million members. Set up in every neighborhood in 1960 to root out counter-revolutionaries, the CDRs' role is broader these days. While they still play a vital role in involving Cubans actively in the defense of the Revolution in its broadest terms — bussing people off to help with the sugar harvest or to practice military drills — they are also engaged in community projects such as vaccination campaigns. Nevertheless, the CDRs are best known for their role as a civilian spy network, keeping tabs (and files) on the personal life and political activities of the local inhabitants.

The Men in Green

The regime which is said to have contemplated abolishing the army after the Revolution now boasts one of Latin America's largest armed forces. The presence of an aggressive neighbor to the north provided reason enough for Cuba to build up its military might. Drumming up hostility against the U.S. and playing on traditional nationalist passion for the *patria* or homeland have been central to the militarization of the Cuban people. From an early age Cubans learn to regard the guerrillas who fought in the Sierra Maestra as epitomes of revolutionary virtue. Even so, many young men feel only loathing for the compulsory military service, on which the regime relies for almost half of its 200,000 regular troops.

In addition, according to official figures, Cuba has a people's militia made up of some 1.3 million men and women. Traditionally, they and many other ordinary citizens (including children) have taken part in basic military training – so that at any one time the leadership could claim that Cuba had over six million people trained and orgnaized to defend the country. Such an active voluntary army has been impossible to maintain during the Special Period.

The financial crisis has forced huge reductions in Cuba's military capability; symbolically, on May 1, 1993, the traditional parade through the Plaza de la Revolución consisted of soldiers riding past on bicycles rather than the usual exhibition of military hardware. The financial crisis has hit the armed forces at a more human level too. The tales of meager food rations within the army have given weight to rumors of discontent in the ranks, but there is no evidence of a serious challenge to the authority of Raúl Castro. Fidel Castro is Commander-in-Chief of the Armed Forces, but as Defense Minister, his brother Raúl oversees the day-to-day command of the military. The siblings together personify the intimate link between the armed forces and political power. The vast majority of army officials belong to the Party, and several high-ranking officers are members of the Politburo.

Raúl Castro is a rather puny figure alongside his brother Fidel, but he is a tireless military leader and has done well to maintain the loyalty of the armed forces. Raúl has also spearheaded the army's increased involvement in tourism, industry, and agricultural production, helping to shore up Cuba's decrepit economy.

Pressure to Conform

Fidel Castro's regime seems mild in comparison with some of Latin America's more notorious twentieth-century dictatorships. There are no death squads, and there is no evidence of systematic torture and police brutality. What exists in Cuba is more of a sophisticated ideological suppression, justified politically as the subordination of the rights of the individual to those of society as a whole. The official line is that personal sacrifices are essential if Cuba is to defend its Revolution against U.S. aggression and preserve the system that supplies such benefits as free healthcare and education, considered by the regime to be the most fundamental human rights. The big question is whether the loss of personal freedom is a justifiable sacrifice.

That the mass organizations have such a large membership, that the turn-out for the 1998 elections was over 98 percent, that Raúl and Fidel Castro both received 99 percent approval from voters in those same elections, these are evidence more of the pressure to conform — or being seen to conform — than of unquestioning support for the system. Anyone can join a mass organization, and only by doing so can they prove their revolutionary credentials. Cubans who refuse to "integrate" politically may find their chosen career barred to them or promotion refused. The price paid for political indifference, let alone dissent, is a black mark on their dossier, which may be consulted when they apply for a new job or if they get into trouble with the authorities.

During the Special Period, Cubans have become increasingly open about discussing the economic hardships, but they are unlikely to openly criticize the system unless they are confident that everyone present is of the same opinion. The weight of the law bears down more heavily on those guilty of active political dissent. The most common charge used to imprison someone who expresses opposition is of disseminating "enemy propaganda," which can include anything from talking to a foreign journalist to distributing subversive leaflets, and carries a sentence of up to eight years. Others have been imprisoned under the charge of *peligrosidad* or "dangerousness," a concept used to punish "anti-social" behavior, and which targets anyone who threatens the social or political order. The charge has been used to remove disaffected youth and other potential trouble-makers from circulation, particularly black marketeers, who are viewed not just as a threat to the national economy but as a more general corrupting influence on society. Conviction usually results in a sentence of one to four years in an agricultural work camp.

The Security Apparatus

When Fidel Castro came to power, there were fifteen prisons on the island. There are now more than 300. The regime justifies high levels of security by pointing to threats, internal and external, to the Revolution. Its critics accuse it of systematically repressing its citizens. The government boasts a simple but sinister system of surveillance in the shape of the CDRs — the main channel through which information reaches the authorities about the views of its citizens. Their work is supplemented by undercover informants (known as *vigilantes*) and *Brigadas de Respuesta Rápida* (Rapid Response Brigades), which are nothing short of organized mobs that intimidate dissidents by laying siege to their homes. Potential troublemakers normally end up in the hands of the Ministry of the Interior (MININT), which is in charge of preserving law and order and deploys all-in-blue police by the thousand. MININT's Department of State Security, set up originally by the KGB and the East German Stasi, deals with dissidents. Harassment by the police, including short-term arrests without charge, tends to rise and fall depending on the level of confidence of the regime.

The system of justice has been criticized by the human rights organization, Amnesty International. Defendants are normally given access to a lawyer only after the investigation has been completed, and sometimes only days or even hours before the court hearing. Cuban law prohibits the use of violence in interrogations, but does allow for "persuasion and convincing." Amnesty asserts that prisoners are often held in cells with no natural light, are interrogated at any time of the day or night, and are pressurized into signing false statements.

The number of political prisoners in Cuban jails remains one of the government's best kept secrets, but the number of prisoners of conscience is estimated to be between 500 and 750. Following the Pope's visit in 1998, it was announced that 300 prisoners would be released, but only a small proportion of these were prisoners of conscience. The regime's cooperation with UN human rights observers has been patchy, largely because Havana believes UN reports to be heavily U.S.-influenced and thus politically motivated. Representatives of Amnesty International are not granted visas to visit Cuba.

Dissident Groups

Fidel Castro insists that the vast majority of Cubans remain loyal to the regime. In reality, it is hard to say how much support it has. Some Cubans hide their feelings beneath a veneer of revolutionary loyalty. Others show discontent by referring to the President as "Castro" rather than the traditional and affectionate "Fidel," or, more boldly, as the "Barbarian" (*Bárbaro*) or "Red Devil" (*Diablo Rojo*). But few Cubans take the step of joining any of the opposition organizations. Many are either bored by politics or are too busy simply surviving. Emigration (legal or illegal) has always been the most effective gesture of disapproval.

The assiduous work of the CDRs and security forces keeps clandestine political activity to a minimum. Many potential leaders of the anti-Castro movement in Cuba have fled the country. However, the recent trend for forging coalitions (with titles even more confusing than those of Cuba's governing bodies) has increased the impact of the 50-odd small and scattered opposition groups. Most of these have emerged since the United Nations Human Rights Commission sent a delegation to the island in 1988. Castro traditionally describes all of them as mere putty in the hands of right-wing Miami exiles, but most are increasingly reasonable in their demands for peaceful dialogue and democratic elections. They believe that many Cubans want peaceful change and not an overthrow of the present regime. They want to retain the gains of the revolution but create spaces for a wider diversity of opinion.

The Democratic Socialist Current (CSD) has a particularly high profile, partly due to the fact that one of its founder members is Elizardo Sánchez. Formerly a professor of Marxist philosophy, Sánchez broke with the Revolution in the 1960s, spent a total of eight years in prison, and is now Cuba's most famous dissident. He has been attacked by both communists and anti-Castroists for his message of reconciliation. Sánchez is also one of the few opposition figures in Cuba to openly contemplate reform with Castro still in place. He claims that the government would certainly be defeated if free elections were held, but that some 20–30 percent of the population would still willingly vote for the Communist Party.

U.S.-Cuban Relations

Wayne Smith, former head of the U.S. diplomatic mission in Havana, once said that Cuba has the same effect in Washington that the full moon has on werewolves: rational behavior ceases at the mere mention of the place. Fidel Castro reserves his most strident language for attacking the U.S., but most people find it easier to comprehend his anger than to understand Washington's obsession with crushing the small nation that dangles from its southern shore.

The events of August 1994, when Castro called off the coastguards and allowed anyone who could put together a raft to leave, was typical of the relationship between Cuba and the U.S., in which Havana calls the shots. The Cuban leader has so far succeeded in foxing nine U.S. presidents, including those who started out with good intentions. President Jimmy Carter opened talks with Havana in 1978, after which Cuban émigrés were allowed to travel back to the island for the first time, and even established limited diplomatic relations. But the Mariel boatlift in 1980 left him looking almost as foolish as Kennedy did after the Bay of Pigs invasion.

More than any of his predecessors, Bill Clinton has had to battle with the contradictions inherent in White House policy towards the island. With the Cold War over, the U.S. restored ties with China and Vietnam, made Yeltsin's Russia a pet project, and is talking to arch-communist North Korea. Yet Washington refuses to compromise over Cuba, even though the embargo has proved effective only in deepening the misery of the Cuban people and providing Castro with a convincing excuse for his country's problems. Vindictive U.S. policy ensures too that the Cuban leader can continue to count on a sizeable body of support among a fiercely patriotic population.

Many Cuban-Americans, particularly the younger generations, are losing patience with their government's blinkered approach to Cuba. Polls show that strong majorities (92 percent of Cuban Americans over 65, and 65 percent of those under 45) still support the embargo, but most people support the exclusion of medical and food supplies — a move also backed by many U.S. businessmen and political figures. Furthermore, a poll in 1997 by the Institute of Public Opinion in Miami found that 51.6 percent (and 77 percent of those aged 18–29) supported the idea of negotiations with Cuba. People are already defying the Trading with the Enemy Act, which bans most Americans from traveling to the island: of the estimated 84,000 U.S. citizens who visited Cuba in 1997, about 20 percent of them did so illegally. Only one man has ever gone to jail for breaching the Trading with the Enemy Act — an indication that the White House is fully aware of how controversial any prosecutions under the Act would be.

Furthermore, there is virtually no support for the embargo abroad: in 1997, 143 countries in the UN General Assembly voted in favor of the resolution against the embargo, compared with just three against (U.S., Israel, and Uzbekistan) and 17 abstentions. The same resolution is presented to the UN annually, and Cuba always wins. The voting figures for the same resolution in 1992 — 59 in favor, three against, and 71 abstentions — show the growing isolation of Washington on the matter.

The White House is under no illusions that its Cuban policy is popular. Moderate politicians in both Republican and Democratic parties, including President Clinton, initially rejected the Helms-Burton Bill, aimed at punishing overseas companies for trading with Cuba. The bill was eventually passed (incomplete) in 1996, but only due to the anti-Castro hysteria which followed the shooting down of the Brothers to the Rescue aircraft (see page 34). U.S. entrepreneurs complain bitterly that competitors from Europe and elsewhere are being allowed to establish a strong foothold in the Cuban market — an area that would otherwise naturally be dominated by U.S. business interests.

Washington argues that calling off the embargo unilaterally could give a new lease of life to Fidel Castro. But it is unlikely that he would be able to control the impact of a flood of North American money, people, and values. Given that the embargo patently has not succeeded in its ostensible aim of bringing democracy to Cuba, it is hard for Washington to defend its position. The continuation of the sanctions is due partly to domestic politics — being tough on Cuba wins the votes of (and donations from) exiles in Miami — but also simply to pride. Such is the history of relations between the U.S. and Cuba that neither leader seems willing to make the first move. As long as the embargo is in place Castro is extremely unlikely to make any political concessions to the US directly — simply out of principle. Likewise, after a stand-off of nearly 40 years, Bill Clinton is reluctant to go down in history as the U.S. President that gave in to Castro. Ironically, he would receive considerable praise around the world for doing just that.

Cuban rafters await rescue by US coastguard, 1994   *C. Brown/Saba-Rea*

Cubans in Exile

Cuban émigré communities exist from Spain to Costa Rica, but the majority of exiles — estimated at around 1.5 million — have settled in the U.S., mostly in Florida and New Jersey. Contacts between Cubans in the two countries are strong. Every year, thousands of Cubans now resident in the U.S. visit relatives on the island and send as much as $300 million to friends and family back home.

It is tempting to regard the one million-plus Cubans who live in Miami as a homogenous mass, but there are many layers to the community. Many waves of Cubans have arrived in Florida since the original exodus in 1959. Those white landowners and businessmen who were the first to flee after the Revolution, and have since amassed large fortunes, are as prejudiced against the black and working-class Cubans in Miami as they were in Cuba before 1959. But many others have been economic migrants seeking the freedom to improve their standard of living and take part in North American consumption culture. They do not consider themselves political refugees and are not interested in the rabid right-wing opposition based in Miami.

Of the various, and predominantly right-wing, political groupings among the Cuban Americans, the most vocal is the Cuban-American National Foundation (CANF). Its 5,000 members, mostly rich businessmen, not only support the embargo but favor a full-blown blockade, and will clearly not be satisfied until Castro has been forced from office. The group has already drawn up its own "blueprint for a free-market economy in a post-Castro

Cuba," which appears to envisage the island as a free-enterprise, semi-client state along the lines of Puerto Rico.

CANF managed to acquire enormous clout in Washington during the 1980s by helping to deliver many of the Cuban-American votes to the government. It was instrumental in getting the Torricelli and Helms-Burton bills approved by Congress in 1992 and 1995 respectively. The group's success was largely thanks to the determination and charisma of its chairman, the late Jorge Mas Canosa. Some have even gone so far as to claim that relations with Cuba might have improved if it had not been for him. He stood alongside President Bush at the signing of the Torricelli Bill, and during the mass emigration of 1994, Bill Clinton even asked him to the White House to discuss how to deal with the crisis. Immediately after Canosa's death from cancer in 1997, there was speculation that CANF would adopt a less extreme position, but the party leaders have so far shown themselves to be committed to maintaining their hard-line approach.

Direct Action

Ever since 1959, enemies of Fidel Castro have adopted extreme measures in order to try and topple him. The CIA no longer sponsors ridiculous assassination attempts against the Cuban leader, but there are others willing to have a go. As recently as 1997, the U.S. coastguard in Puerto Rico detained four Cuban exiles in a boat (said to be owned by a director of CANF) with weapons that were apparently to be used in an attempt on Fidel Castro's life during a visit to Venezuela. Mostly, however, propaganda and harassment are the principal tactics used by right-wingers in Miami. Since the 1980s, Radio and TV Martí have broadcast anti-Castro propaganda across the Florida Straits from Miami, but to little avail since the Cuban government is generally successful in jamming both signals.

The work of the Brothers to the Rescue outfit has been more controversial. Originally set up in Florida to fly out over the Straits to pick up Cuban refugees, when the flow of rafters stopped following the change in U.S. policy on refugees in 1995, the Brothers to the Rescue turned to more direct action against the Cuban government. Pilots began flying provocatively into Cuban airspace, on one occasion buzzing past the Havana seafront, and in 1996 dropping anti-government leaflets over the capital. Following veiled threats of retaliation from Havana, and a number of Cuban efforts to persuade U.S. authoroties to ground the planes, events came to a head in February 1996, when Cuban jets shot down two light aircraft, killing four pilots in the process. Havana has persistently claimed they were in Cuban territory — a suggestion hotly denied by Washington.

Direct action by the exile community against the Castro regime got even closer to home in 1997. In the summer of that year, there were bomb attacks on several Havana hotels, one of which killed an Italian tourist. Cubans in Miami spread the word that the bombs had been planted by underground cells within Cuba, suggesting that members of the armed forces or MININT may have been responsible. The investigation revealed, however, that the

operation had been organized from Miami by a subversive group belonging to CANF. The Salvadorean mercenary captured by the Cuban police confessed to having been paid thousands of dollars to mount the bombing campaign.

As time progresses, right-wing groups such as CANF appear increasingly out of touch with the general mood of the American public. While most Miami exiles want to see the back of Fidel Castro, not all of them are motivated by business interests. The majority are concerned above all about the well-being of families and friends in Cuba; and some, however much they dislike Castro, even see the wisdom of negotiating with the regime. An increasingly influential voice among Cuban exiles is that of Eloy Gutierrez Menoyo, who fought alongside Fidel and Che Guevara in the Sierra Maestra. Polls show that his center-ground democratic group called "Cuban Change" has the support of over 50 percent of exiled Cubans in Miami. He represents a new, moderate faction that recognizes the fact that many Cubans still support Castro.

That Fidel Castro has made the effort to meet (moderate) exile leaders such as Menoyo shows the Cuban leader's awareness that many Cuban Americans are likely to return to the island once the embargo is lifted. Polls in the U.S. produce widely ranging figures, but it is suggested that 20-30 percent of exiles would return to a post-Castro Cuba. On the island itself, there is a real fear that should Castro's regime fall, Cuba could be swamped by U.S. and Cuban-American interests, marginalizing the Cubans who have stuck it out at home and been left destitute by the Special Period. Some are justifiably concerned that that they will be forced out of their homes by pre-1959 owners.

Put simply, Cubans have no desire to replace Castro's Communist Party with a bunch of rich Miami exiles. The only thing most Cubans would accept from the Americans is their money. Not even Fidel Castro himself would reject the exiles' financial help, and he has already held discussions with some exile leaders regarding investment opportunities in the island.

The World View

Of all the guests at Nelson Mandela's inauguration as South Africa's president in 1994, Fidel Castro received the most rapturous welcome. The mystique of the Cuban Revolution, which abroad has not been dulled by the grind of hardship, still arouses genuine affection for its leader. *Granma*, Cuba's Communist Party paper, prints daily messages of solidarity from around the world: gestures of support for the defiant stand by a small nation against the world's only superpower. Humanitarian aid pours in from overseas, with substantial donations from Spain, Germany, Canada, and even organizations in the U.S. The EU alone sends about $20 million in aid annually. For years, brigades of volunteers from all over the world have flown in to assist with construction work and coffee and other harvests.

Taking a joint stand on how the global trading position fails   *AP Photo/Patrick Aviolat*
developing countries, Fidel Castro and Nelson Mandela,
World Trade Organization, 1998

The world's treatment of Castro's regime has traditionally been shaped by pressure from the U.S. government. After Cuba was thrown out of the Organization of American States in 1964, because of arm-twisting by Washington, all member states broke off diplomatic relations, except for Mexico, which has proved to be one of Castro's most faithful allies. The tables are now turning, however, as Latin American nations have become increasingly vocal in their opposition to the embargo. Gradually bonds are being repaired and diplomatic relations restored. The Helms-Burton Bill sparked fury against the U.S. throughout the world, at the same time arousing sympathy for the regime in Havana. The bill even provoked Canada and the EU into threatening legal action against the U.S.

Relations with Spain, the ex-colonial power, have traditionally been good: even under General Franco. The Spanish prime minister succeeded in fouling the friendship in 1997 by criticizing the one-party system and Cuba's human rights record, but the two governments have patched things up, and there is even talk of a possible visit by King Juan Carlos. He would be the first Spanish monarch ever to visit the island.

Havana is fast becoming one of *the* places to be seen, and Fidel Castro's diary must be booked up with appointments with celebrities and foreign dignitaries. The novelist Alice Walker, fashion guru Jean Paul Gaultier, supermodel Naomi Campbell, and Louis Farrakhan, leader of the Nation of Islam, are among recent visitors. All such meetings are a great boost to Fidel Castro's morale, but the visit to beat all visits was undoubtedly that of the Pope.

Several international newspapers described the meeting of Pope John Paul II and Fidel Castro in January 1998 as the "Clash of the Titans." Many observers made the point prior to the visit that Castro was taking a huge risk by inviting the Pope to Cuba: it could, they suggested, galvanize opposition to the regime and spark demonstrations by the Cuban people in the full view of the world's media. If it was a gamble, it paid off. The Pope claimed that the trip was purely pastoral, but also said that he hoped the visit would make Cuba a more just and united country. Once on Cuban soil, he openly criticized the "limitations on fundamental freedoms," and called for the release of political prisoners. Fidel Castro denied that he was hoping to reap any political benefit from the visit, but he used the Pope's open criticism of the embargo (nothing new, in fact) to portray the visit as a defeat for the U.S.

In more general terms, Castro almost certainly hoped to gain respectability for his regime by receiving the world's moral leader. Time will tell whether the visit was a turning point in the history of the Revolution.

Whither Cuba?

In 1993, Castro declared that "capitalism is a failure which offers no future whatsoever to humanity." In a painful ideological contortion, he proceeded to use capitalist measures to save Cuban socialism. He made it clear, however, that the government was whittling away at the communist economic system purely through necessity.

Several years on, the debate rages about how far the regime will go along the route of free enterprise in order to save the Revolution. After a whole range of reforms, introduced from 1993–5, which helped steer Cuba away from economic oblivion, more recently the emphasis has been placed on continuity, in both political and economic terms.

In politics, it is clear that the regime wants to stick with the single-party system and shore up the socialist system come what may. During government reshuffles, the old *históricos* (those of Fidel Castro's generation) are gradually being replaced by younger blood, in an attempt to guarantee the survival of revolutionary politics into the next millennium.

As far as economic measures are concerned, the evidence is that the government wishes to limit liberalization, focusing instead on improving efficiency of the existing system. According to some observers, this is not so much due to Fidel Castro's determination to prevent the re-emergence of the bourgeoisie, which the Revolution has fought so hard to destroy, but due to his fear of losing political control. The fact is that the Cubans who have gone into private business have discovered that they can get on much better without government interference. If Cubans no longer need the government to tell them what to do, how will the regime hold onto their loyalty? In the opinion of dissident Elizardo Sánchez, with the economy and *Fidelismo* in tatters, the security apparatus is the only thing Castro can rely on to keep control of his people.

The Leadership

The prediction of Castro's demise has been a favorite pastime ever since the Berlin Wall fell in 1989. The Cuban leader has proved adept both at outliving his political obituaries and at tantalizing speculators about his future. His declaration in 1994 that "revolutionaries do not retire," was followed some months later by a statement saying that if the Americans lifted the embargo he would resign.

It is difficult to imagine Fidel Castro standing down; any subsequent leader would be hard pushed to command any authority as long as he was still alive. However, it seems that Castro is at least trying to ensure an orderly transition after he is gone, aware that his sudden disappearance from the scene could result in political turmoil.

At the Communist Party Congress in 1997, the Cuban leader declared on record for the first time that Raúl Castro, Defense Minister, was his designated successor. "Raúl has more youth and more energy than me," he declared, "he has more time ahead of him." Since then, Raúl has assumed a wider range of official duties and is playing a more prominent and more varied role in the running of the government, perhaps, it has been suggested, as part of a strategy to accustom ordinary Cubans to the idea that he will eventually be their next leader. People have assumed for years that Raúl would succeed, but he is not popular among ordinary Cubans. He lacks the charisma of his elder brother and has the reputation of being a political hard-liner. While he is generally thought of as being more pragmatic on economic issues than Fidel, he is probably even more dogmatic when it comes to ideology; he was attracted to communism long before Fidel was.

From now on, the words and actions of Raúl are likely to arouse almost as much interest as those of his brother. Some observers are already interpreting Raúl's push to increase the army's role in running the economy (the army virtually controls the sugar industry and it has a big interest in the tourism business) as part of a general campaign to increase the power of the military. Its loyalty would be crucial in the event of political turmoil, particularly if Fidel Castro were no longer on the scene.

The rise of Raúl and the military could also be interpreted as a signal that the influence of reform-minded members of the government is on the wane. However, two such men, who have come to the fore during the Special Period, seem certain to be influential in any future government. The first is

Carlos Lage, a cautious technocrat in charge of the economy, whose role has expanded to the extent where he now supervises much of the day-to-day administration of the government; and Ricardo Alarcón, the sharp-tongued, sharp-witted president of the National Assembly, who is the more charismatic of the two and has shown himself to be a skilful negotiator abroad. Plascon, a former ambassador the the UN, has maintained control of U.S.-Cuban relations even while someone else has led the Foreign Ministry. People once talked of Roberto Robaina, who became Foreign Minister in 1993 aged just 37, as a potential successor to Fidel Castro, but he is perceived as being little more than Fidel's puppet and enjoys little respect among the people outside his own significant political base in the Union of Young Communists.

It seems unlikely that reformers will be sidelined as long as Fidel Castro is alive, but there is no guarantee that if Fidel goes, opposing political factions would not vie for power. Raúl might have the army behind him, but reformers could well have the people on their side.

Castro or Chaos

"And if, in order to crush the Revolution, they have to kill all the people, the people, behind its leaders and its Party, will be willing to die!" The kind of faithful revolutionaries who energize the rallies over which Fidel Castro presides would probably not hesitate to defend their country to the end. But the desperation with which Cubans fled in 1994 suggested how many people would also rather die leaving by raft than fighting to defend the system. Many would also rather leave than fight against the system. There is no great stomach for rebellion in Cuba. Many fear that a popular uprising would lead to bloody civil strife as years of frustration and hatred would explode and pitch Cubans against one another. And what would the alternative be? Impoverished chaos seems a more realistic prospect than well-off liberal democracy, a political system Cubans have never known.

A mixture of patriotism, distrust of the Miami émigrés, and sheer resilience may partly explain the Revolution's survival. However bad things are now, the old revolutionaries say, they were infinitely worse under Batista. But more than half of all Cubans have been born since the Revolution and take their still-egalitarian education and healthcare for granted, and people say that few of them support the regime. They are bored by the system and the unchanging face of the leadership, and are hungry for consumer goods and a chance to live their lives to the full. The future of Cuba lies in their hands.

4 ECONOMY: STATE AND MARKET

"We have no reason to create millionaires."
— Fidel Castro, 1997

Cuba's resources suggest that it should easily be the strongest economy in the Caribbean. Agricultural potential is strong; its mineral wealth is significant; and its share of the world's biggest industry, tourism, should be the largest of any Caribbean island. Furthermore, the labor force is every investor's dream: young, healthy, and highly educated. Instead, Cuba has spent years trying to avoid disappearance into what one government economist once described as "an economic Bermuda Triangle."

So what went wrong? At a time when virtually all other nations around the world (some with strong ideological reluctance) were moving towards free-market reform, Fidel Castro refused to permit private enterprise. For years, he could afford to preside over a grossly inefficient economy because of the enormous subsidy provided by the USSR. Since 1990, however, the island has had to fight to keep its head above water. The embargo has been held responsible for the near-collapse of Cuba's economy, but it could be argued that the U.S. has simply twisted a knife which was already deeply embedded. Ironically, the fact that the country continues to function at all is due in large part to the remittances sent by Cuban exiles in the U.S. to relatives on the island, and which are said to be worth over $300 million a year.

A Tale of Two Superpowers

Prior to 1959, Cuba was effectively owned and operated as a subsidiary of the U.S. Investment in everything from sugar to illicit sex originated in North America. The economy generally performed well but always in an extraordinarily iniquitous fashion. The workforce was exploited, profits repatriated, and the island's infrastructure engineered for the benefit of foreign interests. Anger at this economic colonization was one reason why the Revolution's expropriation of North American assets in the 1960s received such popular backing in Cuba. Not in Washington, however, which still claims that Cuba nationalized some $8 billion worth of U.S.-owned property without adequate compensation.

The Cold War enabled the revolutionaries to get by without their northern neighbor. The political shift to communism mirrored the economic move into the Soviet sphere of influence. By joining an economic world that was independent of the U.S., Cuba could wriggle free of the constraints imposed by the embargo. When, in 1976, Cuba joined COMECON (the communist common market), it plugged into a system where it could make a unique contribution. East Germany got fresh fruit, Czechoslovaks could take

Caribbean holidays, and Soviet citizens from Vilnius to Vladivostok enjoyed Cuban sugar.

Sugar-cane was at the root of the deal with the USSR. Moscow guaranteed Cuba a price for its harvest. Not only was this usually well above the world price, but it also gave the economy a degree of stability unknown to the rest of the commodity-dependent Caribbean. Payment was made in oil at a price both predictable and well below the going rate, and Cuba was free to sell the surplus on the world market. Thanks to this deal worth $5 billion a year, Cuba could fuel its development and feed, educate, and treat its people. Bread made from Soviet wheat formed part of Cubans' daily diet, and consumer goods were widely available, even if they were often of only poor quality.

Despite good intentions, Cuba's communist regime has not been good for the economy. The inability of such a fertile tropical island to feed its population, for example, is due primarily to the communist obsession with centralization and of management based more on improvisation than long-term planning. Since virtually all economic activity was run by the government, there was no pressure for state enterprises to make a profit. This inefficient state of affairs did not really matter as long as the USSR could make up the shortfall: before communism collapsed, more than 70 percent of Cuba's foreign trade was with the USSR, and another 15 percent with the rest of the Eastern bloc.

At the January 1990 COMECON meeting, it was recognized that economic ties between Moscow and Havana would continue, but that transactions were to be made in hard currency. The USSR massively reduced its levels of support to Cuba and GDP plummeted. By 1992, structural reforms were being introduced. Institutions were forced to justify themselves economically as the steady supply of cash from the central planning authorities slowly dried up. Ministries were obliged to seek their own ways of earning hard currency; even the armed forces and the Union of Young Communists started dabbling in tourism.

Liberalization

In July 1993, Castro announced that Cuba's imports had fallen from over $8 billion in 1989 to a mere $2.2 billion in 1992. Drastic action had to be taken. The government began streamlining state firms, eliminating some and merging others. The subsidies that had cushioned Cubans, and kept prices at levels almost unchanged since the 1960s, were slowly stripped away from transport, telephone services, fuel, alcohol, and tobacco. The most controversial card to be played, however, was the decriminalization of the dollar. Previously, the only Cubans allowed to use dollars were a few privileged citizens, including Party officials. If the legalization of the dollar demonstrated that the government could not control the black market, it meant that at least it could start to siphon off some of the money circulating within it. In Havana, new dollar shops seemed to open on a daily basis, each with a line stretching down the block. Food apart, the things most Cubans wanted to buy could be found only at the hard currency stores.

In September 1993, Decree Law 141 lifted the virtual state monopoly of production and employment by authorizing limited private enterprise in a range of more than 100 trades from hairdressing to shoe repairs. By 1997, there were over 170,000 registered self-employed workers, the majority involved in the retail and catering trades — hence the proliferation of street traders and private restaurants

A bare shop window in Havana   *Emily Hatchwell*

called *paladares*. In 1994, the government made an equally significant concession with the introduction of farmers' markets for the sale of fresh produce at deregulated prices.

The opening up of Cuba to foreign investment has been the other major innovation. Constitutional changes have made it possible for overseas companies to invest in virtually every sector of the economy, except national security, defense, education, and public health. The magazine *Business Tips on Cuba*, sold on the island, carries scores of advertisements by Cuban factories and other enterprises in search of a foreign partner. Initially, overseas firms were allowed no more than a 50 percent stake in any "joint venture," but since 1995 they can obtain full ownership. Such enterprises are independent of government control and are permitted to export their own products and repatriate their profits.

There are currently over 250 joint ventures in operation, involving 50 countries, with several hundred more under discussion. Mexico is Cuba's leading foreign investor. Other countries with big investment interests include Canada, Spain, and Italy. Investment is heaviest in the fields of tourism, mining, and oil, with growing interest also shown in communications and energy.

The Helms-Burton Bill, aimed at discouraging foreign investment in Cuba (see p00), triggered the withdrawal of several companies from Cuba soon after it was introduced, but otherwise its impact has been minimal. More of a discouragement to foreign investors is the amount of red tape they have to deal with, and the other restrictions imposed on them. Running an efficient, profit-making business in a country which still rallies to the call "Socialism or Death!" is not without its pitfalls.

Parallel Economies

A good indication of the economic well-being of any nation is provided by its currency. Officially, the Cuban peso is on a par with the U.S. dollar. In 1989, its value on the black market was around five pesos to one dollar. By 1994 this had fallen to 120 pesos. Several years on, the government has helped restore the value of the national currency to a relatively stable rate of around 20 pesos to the dollar. This is thanks mainly to a series of reforms, in particular measures to increase demand for local currency (the opening in 1994 of private farmers' markets alone led to a 470 million-peso rise in domestic sales in just three months) and to tackle the rampant black market in currency: in 1995, official exchange houses called *Cadecas* were introduced, permitting Cubans to exchange dollars and pesos legally at the free-market rate. The average street rate now parallels that offered at the *Cadecas.*

Cuba also has the *peso convertible,* which has exactly the same value as the dollar and can be used in lieu of the greenback in Cuba. The government introduced the *peso convertible* in order to reduce the "float" of U.S. dollars in circulation. While this currency is not recognized on the world market, the government does hope one day to merge the convertible and non-convertible pesos.

Julio Etchart

Despite the improved status of the peso, the greenback is still the only currency that really counts in Cuba. While the shelves in any shop where goods are sold for Cuban pesos are half empty, dollar shops are chock-a-block with imported consumer goods from shampoo to stereos. The dollar dominates the field of tourism to such an extent that foreign visitors to Cuba can quite easily spend two weeks on the island without handling a single peso.

Cuba's dollar economy is essentially a legal capitalist sector, created by the government when it decriminalized the dollar in 1993, and it is flourishing. So, too, is the black market. The illegal trade in currency has been hit by the setting up of the *Cadecas* and the government's acceptance of the free-market rate of exchange, but the black market in goods is booming. Door-to-door peddlers offer everything from hard-to-obtain foreign goods to home-made cakes. Unlike in other Latin American countries, the black market in Cuba is not the preserve of the marginal classes, but is responsible instead for circulating goods and services among all sectors of society. It is estimated that between 1993 and 1995, people traded as much on the black market as they did in the state sector.

While in the beginning people turned to the black market to obtain basic food supplies, now it is the only option for many people wanting to buy a whole range of goods, particularly those with no access to dollars. People often find better quality goods on the street than in government shops, too, and dollar prices are often lower: two dozen eggs that cost $5 in a dollar store will probably cost just $3 on the street.

Agriculture and Food

After 1959, about three-quarters of Cuba's agricultural land was confiscated from private landowners and converted into vast, Soviet-style state farms. These dominated the countryside for over three decades. The face of the agricultural sector, however, has changed dramatically during the Special Period as a result of measures to stop the plummeting production levels of Cuba's main crops.

Although food supplies are marginally better than during the worst years of the Special Period, from 1992-4, the figures for food production still make depressing reading. According to a 1997 report by the UN Economic Commission for Latin America and the Caribbean, between 1989 and 1995, Cuba's chicken flocks decreased by 58 percent, citrus output fell by 32 percent, milk production by 40 percent and egg production by 52 percent. While Cuba boasted ten million head of cattle in the 1980s, it now has just five or six million: the cows have either starved to death or been killed for food. The latter is considered such a serious offense that Cubans joke that you get more years for killing a cow than for murdering a human being.

Such appalling food shortages, and the fact that more than 40 percent of Cuba's food has to be imported, have forced the government to revolutionize the way food is both produced and sold. The most significant change as far as most Cubans are concerned was the reinstatement of farmers' markets in 1994, which allowed farmers to sell their surplus produce direct to the people at prices determined by supply and demand rather than by the state. To some extent this simply legalized the informal market which already existed, but the move has encouraged the cultivation of land which was left out of production for years due to the low prices for crops offered by the state. These markets have greatly boosted the amount of fresh produce available, but most Cubans must scrape to afford the prices charged at these markets: a pound of ham can cost as much as a week's wages. And they have not led to an increase in the quantity of food provided by the state via the ration book, or *libreta,* which remains insufficient.

Fuel shortages mean that sugar production
depends on antiquated techonology

Emily Hatchwell

More significantly for the economy, the Cuban government has also accepted that the state sector simply cannot manage the land as effectively as private farmers and cooperatives. By 1997, the state has reduced its control of agricultural land to just 25 percent, down from 75 percent in 1992, although it maintains some control by setting annual production quotas. Since 1993, underused areas of arable land belonging to state farms have been turned into so-called Basic Units of Cooperative Production (UBPCs), where members have the right to use the land and own the fruit of their labor. These now account for over a third of Cuba's arable land. Figures published in *Granma* have revealed that only about 40 percent of UBPCs are profitable, but such cooperatives have still helped boost production of many crops.

Cuba is one of the world's top producers of sugar, which has been the island's most significant crop since the early colonial period. Sugar-cane still covers more than 50 percent of cultivated land. The oil-for-sugar swap arrangement, brokered with the USSR following the Revolution, seemed beneficial so long as Cuba was producing as much as seven million tons of sugar a year, but left the island devastated when the Soviet Union disintegrated. Firstly, the oil-for-sugar trade locked the island into a monoculture of a commodity that today has no guaranteed market and offers fluctuating prices. Secondly, the sugar industry, which became almost totally mechanized after 1959, was devastated by the shortages of fuel and spare parts that followed the withdrawal of Soviet support. The harvests in 1996 and 1997 yielded 4.4 and 4.2 million tons respectively, compared with the pre-1989 average of almost double that.

The Cuban government seems determined to boost the sugar harvest to the old levels. Bad weather and shortages have hampered recovery, but the main issues that must be tackled are poor organization and inefficiency. Millions of dollars are needed to modernize Cuba's decrepit sugar mills. Foreign money is already lined up, but it is likely that some mills may have to close — a politically sensitive move since some rural communities are completely dependent on them as a source of employment. An overhaul of the industry will be welcomed in other quarters: recent harvests have relied heavily on the army and on the large-scale mobilization of students and workers from the cities.

The shortage of agricultural labor affects the entire agricultural sector. The shortfall is largely the result of the improvement in services in the towns since the Revolution, which brought a dramatic population shift from the countryside. Thousands of young men now do obligatory agricultural rather than military service, with perks offered to encourage them to stay on in the countryside afterwards and marry local women. The so-called *Plan Turquino* was set up some time ago in an attempt to repopulate Cuba's mountainous areas, in particular to aid the production of coffee in the Sierra Maestra.

Much to the chagrin of most Cubans, for whom it is a passion, coffee is one of the country's largest agricultural exports, leaving little for local ration books. Nor do they see as much of the island's most celebrated product, tobacco (most of which grows in the western province of Pinar del Río) as they'd like to. The fashion for cigar-smoking around the world has given a welcome boost to Cuba's export sales: around 100 million cigars were exported in 1997, contributing around $170 million to the state coffers. The boom has inspired the creation of several new brands of cigar, too, including the Cuaba, launched in 1996, and the Vegas Robaina, launched in 1997. These, like the famous Cohiba cigar, are strictly for export.

Cuba's other principal crops include rice, beans, and citrus fruit.

Biotechnology and Pharmaceuticals

One doesn't automatically think of Cuba, traditionally reliant on agriculture for the bulk of its revenue, as being a great manufacturing nation. Industrial products include paper, timber, processed food and drink, cement, and textiles, but industry has never been Cuba's strong point, and few foreign companies have shown an interest in bailing out the island's out-of-date and poorly run industrial plants. There are two areas in which the country has made great strides over the last two decades, however, and that is in biotechnology and pharmaceuticals.

These industries have developed both out of the need to counter the effects of the embargo on medical supplies and also as a means to diversify the economy. Almost $150 million was spent on the construction of Havana's Center of Genetic Engineering and Biotechnology, opened in 1986, and Cuban scientists have done pioneering research in several fields: tests for an anti-AIDS vaccine began in 1996, making Cuba one of just six nations in the world to begin clinical tests on humans.

Given that the price of sugar and other raw materials produced in Cuba is generally low, the regime has been prudent in its decision to invest in biotechnology. Progress in the field of research has been such as to enable Cuba not only to serve its own needs but also to look to the export market. The island's pharmaceutical industry is the nation's sixth largest currency earner, contributing around $120 million a year and selling products such as an anti-cholesterol drug called PPG, insulin, and vaccines against meningitis and hepatitis B, primarily to Third World nations. In addition, every year Cuba attracts several thousand foreigners to the island for medical treatment for anything from cancer to chronic neurological disorders.

So far, the government has shown itself to be reluctant to invite foreign investment in this field, but only by doing so is Cuba likely to be able to compete in the developed world, where the market is controlled by Western multinationals.

Oil and Mining

If Fidel Castro could make one wish, it would possibly be for Cuba to discover an oil field to rival Colombia's or Venezuela's. The island already has offshore deposits, mainly along the north coast, but they are small-scale and the oil is of low quality. The high sulfur content means that the oil not only exudes a most unpleasant smell during drilling (which afflicts Cuba's flagship resort, Varadero), but also corrodes the boilers and other components of the power plants. Even so, Cupet, the state oil company, has been increasingly successful in attracting outside investment and domestic oil production climbs slowly.

Foreign interest in oil and mining accounts for about 30 percent of all joint ventures. Nickel, copper, chromium, and gold are the main minerals currently being mined on the island. Nickel is Cuba's most abundant precious mineral and its third highest-earning export after tourism and sugar. It is thought that the island has the world's fourth largest reserves of nickel, mostly in the eastern province of Holguín. After the Revolution, the managers of the largest mines left the country and took the plans with them to try and paralyze further nickel extraction. Soviet assistance helped Cuba overcome such setbacks, but the state sector used inefficient technology. Joint ventures, with the Canadian mining company Sherritt International leading the field, look set to increase production dramatically.

Tourism

Cuba is splendidly endowed to take advantage of the worldwide growth in tourism. It has all the advantages: a tropical location, beautiful beaches, a rich culture, stunning scenery, and a gregarious people.

Foreign investors, to whom the Cuban government has given considerable new flexibility, have poured more money into tourism than into any other sector of the economy. In Varadero, joint ventures between the Cuban government and overseas companies from Mexico, Germany, Spain, and elsewhere have led to the construction of the country's biggest and best hotels. These vast complexes can compete at the top international level but, like many large holiday resorts, are a world away from the "real" Cuba, where more enterprising tourists find atmospheric one-horse towns with echoes of colonial grandeur, architectural gems like Trinidad, and unrivalled tranquillity as in the Viñales valley in western Cuba. Since the big push for tourists focuses on package tourism to the island's beaches, such areas still see comparatively few visitors.

The statistics for the industry look impressive. After a period of neglect during the 1960s and 1970s, tourism is now the fastest growing sector of the economy: it is currently expanding at an annual rate of about 20 percent and earns over $1.5 billion a year. The 326,000 visitors recorded in 1989 rose to over one million in 1997. The country to send the most tourists is Canada, followed by Italy, Germany, Spain, and Mexico.

Despite these successes, the regime's prediction of two million tourists for the year 2000 and possibly ten million by the year 2010 (the same number of tourists already visit the Bahamas every year, and this is a much smaller country) is optimistic. While the industry has now overtaken sugar as Cuba's main source of hard currency, high net earnings are counter-balanced by dependency on expensive, hard-currency imports. Furthermore, the industry remains inefficient and future growth is likely to be limited by the island's poor tourism infrastructure.

The Chinese Example

The foreign minister, Roberto Robaina, spends much of his time flying around the world trying to encourage trade with Cuba. Pressure from Washington on potential business partners has hampered the search for new markets, but links have improved substantially with nations all over the world — from the Caribbean to China and Vietnam.

Because of their political backgrounds, these last two countries are perhaps the best economic models for Cuba to follow. Since they shrugged off state control, both China and Vietnam have harnessed their human potential for intense economic growth. The establishment of free agricultural markets is exactly the sort of move which seems designed to emulate the success stories of Asia. Since his visit to China in 1995, Fidel Castro has spoken admiringly about the result of economic changes there. But he has also made clear that he is opposed to privatizing state enterprises, a step

Improvised public transport

M. O'Brien/Panos

ordered by the Chinese Communist Party at its congress in 1997. Fidel Castro is at pains to emphasize that the situations in the two countries are very different, and that it would not be logical for them to take the same path.

Economic Outlook

Following a decline of 35 percent in its GDP figures between 1990 and 1993, Cuba managed to achieve limited but stable growth for several years, from 0.7 percent in 1994 to 7.8 percent in 1996. However, that figure fell to just 2.5 percent in 1997. Cuba also faces an external debt estimated at $11 billion, a trade deficit of $1.7 billion, and continued shortages of many basic goods. And although trade figures are up for certain commodities, the effect is neutralized by low world prices. Meanwhile, the demand for imports has grown much faster than export earnings, and the cost of fuel and food, which together make up about 70 percent of Cuba's import bill, is very high.

The government cannot afford to admit that its economic policies are not working. It handles public utterances on the state of the economy carefully, so, despite the poor figures, ministers still talked of a sustained recovery and "discrete growth" at the Communist Party Congress in 1997. Speculation that the limited moves towards creating a free-market economy would be extended were dashed as the congress instead supported maintaining the status quo for as long as possible. In fact, recent measures suggest that the government is actually planning to put a stop to capitalist-style measures and even revert to previous models before private businesses gain too much momentum.

Any visitor to Cuba will come across countless examples of how Cubans are better off if they work for themselves: how an engineer who used to make 300 pesos (about $15) a month working for the state is now earning several hundred dollars as a taxi driver; why a teacher retired early so that she could make souvenirs to sell at a local market, and so on.

Castro clearly feels fundamentally uncomfortable with the idea of creating private wealth. When income tax, not seen in Cuba for decades, was introduced on all hard-currency earnings in January 1996, some analysts viewed it not so much as a means to raise revenue but as a means of keeping a lid on private enterprise. Indeed, some have even suggested that the sharp rise in taxes in 1997 was designed to actually wipe private businesses out. A private restaurant or *paladar* can face an income tax bill of as much as $1,000 per month, regardless of the number of meals served and despite the fact that no private restaurant may seat more than twelve people at a time. Many *paladares* have reportedly closed or gone underground.

The leadership must also be concerned that the efficiency of joint ventures and home-grown private enterprise casts the island's state sector in an increasingly poor light, arguably leaving the state in danger of being pushed out by the private sector in certain areas. Everyone recognizes that private restaurants and foreign-run hotels, for example, are generally far better than their state-run counterparts. The improvement in the performance of state enterprises, making them as efficient as those in the dollar economy, is now a government priority.

Efficiency drives usually mean job losses. Unemployment, which was abolished in the 1960s, has now returned to Cuba. Officially, the number of unemployed is put at about 7 percent of the population, but in reality the figure is likely to be much higher. State-run offices are full of workers who can barely fulfill their tasks for lack of resources. And it is said that many people continue going into work simply to be able to steal goods — from ice cream to building materials.

The problem facing the government is that if it does not put the brake on capitalism-inspired reforms, where does it draw the line? If it carries on opening up the economy, pressure will mount, for example, to increase the number of trades open to private enterprise; to allow university graduates, doctors, and others to set up their own businesses (hitherto excluded for fear that they would abandon their poorly-paid state jobs); to pay Cubans at least part of their salaries in dollars – more and more Cubans are desperate to work in tourism for the access it brings to hard currency; as things stand, it is eminently worthwhile for an architect to become a bellhop or a waiter, simply because of the tips they can expect. The dilemma for the government is that while all these measures would improve living conditions for Cubans, they could also ultimately threaten the regime's control.

5 SOCIETY: DIVERSITY AND EQUALITY

"No revolution could be more potent than Cuban eroticism"
— Jacobo Timerman, 1987

Word spreads quickly when food arrives at the local government store. The latest consignment of eggs might be the first the neighborhood has seen for several months. The ration book or *libreta* should guarantee Cubans a regular supply of staple goods, such as rice, beans, cooking oil, and sugar, but the full monthly quota rarely materializes. Rationing in Cuba, introduced in 1962, is supposed to ensure that everyone gets an equal amount of food each month. But the meager rations are no longer nearly enough to live on. Even the men who gather to gossip in the town squares are likely to spend as much time discussing the latest food allowances as the latest baseball scores.

The pressures resulting from the everyday fight for survival are manifested in many different ways, from high divorce and suicide rates to increased alcoholism. People lining up for their daily bread roll discuss ways to make a little extra cash, ways to make shampoo from the sap of a particular cactus. It's all part of *resolviendo* or "getting by." It shows not only the kind of creative spark which has enabled Cubans to endure the economic crisis, but also the strains being placed on human relationships — within both the community and the family.

Ethnic Mix

Dividing Cubans — the greatest racial jumble in the Caribbean — into neat percentages of ethnicity is a hapless activity. Official statistics suggest that the population breaks down as follows: 66 percent white (Hispanic), 12 percent black (descendants of slaves from West Africa and migrants from other Caribbean islands), 21.9 percent mulatto (mixed Hispanic and black) and 0.1 percent Asian. These figures are clearly inaccurate. Some people suggest that as much as 70 percent of the population is *mestizo*, i.e. of mixed European and African ancestry. Cubans with the highest percentage of African blood live in western Cuba, primarily in Havana and nearby Matanzas province.

Cubans as a whole have become decidedly darker since 1959. The economic and social changes brought by the Revolution encouraged unprecedented movement within the population and between races, not only between the towns and country but also between the classes. Furthermore, the majority of the Cubans who have left the country since the 1960s have been white.

After Europe and Africa, China has contributed most to Cuba's racial medley. As many as 150,000 Chinese laborers arrived during the second half of the nineteenth century, mostly to work on the plantations — firstly alongside slaves and later to replace them. Even after abolition, the new arrivals from Asia often lived in conditions that were as appalling as those endured by their predecessors. Later, these same workers or newer immigrants set up their own businesses, from laundries to restaurants, or became farmers. While many considered themselves "Cuban" — it is said that around 6,000 took part in the war of independence — they kept their traditional Chinese costume and traditions. At the time of the Revolution, they had their own school, newspapers in their own language, and several cinemas that showed only Chinese films. Today, the Chinese population is officially put at around 10,000, but this suggests a misleading degree of ethnic purity. Havana's *Barrio Chino* (Chinatown) has dwindled almost to nothing as its inhabitants have died or inter-married, although the quarter has been spruced up recently with the help of government money.

Racial Equality

By many standards, Cuba is a paradise of racial harmony. Black and white kids play together happily, mixed race couples are common, and the kind of racial violence that afflicts Britain and the U.S. is conspicuous by its absence.

In March 1959, Fidel Castro declared that he would eliminate the racial discrimination that had flourished before the Revolution. The new regime was generous with its legislation, opening up areas previously closed to Afro-Cubans, such as beaches, hotels, and universities, and granting them equal rights in the workplace. In 1966, Castro announced that race discrimination had been eradicated.

However, losing a large percentage of Cuba's richest and most racist citizens to the U.S., transforming racism into a taboo subject, and removing the legal pillars of discrimination cannot eliminate prejudice. Athletes and musicians are more likely to be black than white, but whites occupy the upper echelons of most other fields, including government. African and biracial Cubans have many more educational and employment opportunities open to them than they did prior to the Revolution, and at least they share the same healthcare as other Cubans, but there is still progress to be made.

Social marginalization, as in other countries, means that more blacks than whites resort to crime. Young black males are often harassed by the police, particularly in Havana, and some ordinary Cubans will also assume that anyone who has been robbed was the victim of a black criminal.

That a Hispanic girl wanting to marry a black Cuban may on occasion face parental pressure to dissolve the relationship stems partly from historical precedent; in colonial times, while it was perfectly acceptable for a white man to lust after a *mulata*, liaisons between white women and black men were frowned upon. It stems too from the recognition that a black husband has less hope of offering a good home than a white Cuban, as well as from more straightforward prejudice or social snobbery. Equally, black parents tend to consider marriage with a white Cuban as a "good" match.

Religion

Communism has never succeeded in taking the place of religious faith in Cuba. On the other hand, the Catholic Church remains weaker than anywhere else in Latin America. A mixture of persuasion and repression has reduced the number of worshippers since 1959, but the orthodox Catholic Church had scant influence even before the Revolution, when it was seen by many Cubans as being in cahoots with the richest social classes and the ideological ally of corrupt governments.

For many years, practicing Catholics were punished for their religious faith, by being denied access to education and jobs. The relationship between the Catholic Church and the government since then has been one of uneasy coexistence characterized principally by a feeling of mutual distrust. Following the dark days of the 1960s and 1970s, a few conciliatory gestures were exchanged in the 1980s, and the admission of Catholics into the Communist Party in 1991 was seen as a major concession. The commitment to atheism written into the constitution was also dropped. Such developments have not put an end to confrontation; in 1993, an open letter published by Cuban bishops attacked the "omnipresent official ideology" and accused the regime of denying civil rights, but generally the 1990s have seen an improvement in the status of the church. Congregations have grown, churches closed since the 1960s have reopened, and the number of publications printed by the church has risen. The latter are generally just small-scale parish publications, often reproduced on photocopiers, but they are sought after for opinions on economical and social, as well as religious, issues. Suggestions that this proliferation of Catholic media is evidence of an underground Catholic movement are so far unproven.

It is a recognized phenomenon the world over that people turn to religion during times of social or economic crisis. It is suggested that the growth in church attendance, in both Catholic and Protestant denominations, is also a response to the perceived growing moral emptiness of Castroism. The number of baptisms has doubled in the last decade, although of an estimated five million Cubans who are baptized Catholics, only about ten percent of them are practicing.

When the history of the Catholic Church in Cuba is written in years to come, Pope John Paul II's visit to the island in January 1998 could well be portrayed as a milestone in its relationship with the state. The political significance of the Pope's visit aside, the impact of his visit on the status of the church on the island cannot yet fully be assessed. It is clear, however, that both the Pope and Catholic leaders in Cuba hoped it would reinvigorate the church, give worshippers greater freedom to express their beliefs and put an end to confrontation with the regime.

The signs have been promising. In the run-up to the visit, Fidel Castro announced that Christmas Day, abolished in the 1960s, would be an official holiday in 1997, although he also made it clear that this was to be a one time event. Perhaps more significantly for the church, Jaime Ortega, the charismatic archbishop of Havana, became the first Cuban cleric to address the nation on television since 1959. All over the island, priests and bishops held special masses during which they praised the Pope and also explained who he was: many young Cubans who have grown up in the atheist atmosphere of the Revolution had no idea what the Pope represented.

During his visit, which included the usual round of open-air masses, the Pope exhorted the leadership to give greater space to the church, and tabled several specific demands, including that Roman Catholic schools should be reopened. While such a step is unlikely to happen quickly, the church in Cuba is pressing for at least permission to offer religious instruction in Cuban schools. Importantly, the church has already been given permission to build a third seminary, giving it a chance to build up its depleted number of priests. Before the Revolution, there were around 900 priests, whereas now the figure is nearer 250 (less than half of whom are Cuban).

In the presence of the Pope, Fidel Castro declared that "Respect for believers and non-believers is a basic principle that we Cuban revolutionaries have inculcated in our compatriots." Time will tell whether such words spring from the heart or were merely part of a public relations campaign.

The Protestant Church is also likely to benefit from the visit of the Pope, although its relationship with the government is traditionally reasonably good since it has made more effort than its Catholic counterpart to embrace the Revolution. The Baptists figure most prominently among the 70 or so non-Catholic churches, although the world trend for evangelism has reached Cuba too.

Santería

According to a local saying, if you scratch any Cuban Catholic you'll find a follower of *santería*, a blend of African and Catholic beliefs that developed during the colonial period and which is universally acknowledged to have a greater following than Catholicism or any other religion in Cuba. This fusion of beliefs, known as syncretism, was possible largely because colonial landowners made such poor missionaries; they were more interested in their slaves' capacity for work than in their souls. Although the slaves were forbidden to practice their native religions, they managed to hide worship of their own African deities behind the names and images of Catholic saints. During the pretence of Catholic worship, the slaves subsumed aspects of Christian belief into their own religion.

Afro-Cuban culture is most strongly represented in music
Julio Etchart/Reportage

/ Given the Catholic element in *santería*, it is hard to know where one religion ends and the other begins. Indeed, few *santería* believers see much contradiction in following both churches. If you see a Cuban praying in church, can you be sure whether he or she is praying to a Catholic saint or an African god? Such a conundrum helps explain the unreliability of any statistics regarding the number of practicing Catholics in Cuba. Interestingly, *santería* followers come from all racial groups and all walks of life.

The term *santería* is often misused to describe all Afro-Cuban faiths, but it is simply the most widespread. *Santería*, also known as *Regla de Ocha*, evolved from the cult of the Yorubá or Lucumí people of Nigeria. It is not so much a faith as a way of life, in which people's lives are ruled by African deities called *orishas*. If believers have a string of bad luck, they will probably blame it on an *orisha*'s displeasure at some misdemeanor or at their neglect of religious duties. But there is no talk of sin or the final judgment.

Such an apparently irrational and unmoralizing faith would seem anathema to communists, with their scientific conception of the world and often puritanical attitudes, but *santería* attracts even members of the Party (including, they say, Fidel Castro himself). The government has opened museums devoted to *santería* and published a string of books about it, although cynics might suggest that such official promotion is largely dictated by the need to capitalize on the interest shown in Afro-Cuban culture by visiting tourists. In reality, *santería* does not pose the kind of threat to communist orthodoxy that Christianity traditionally does.

Just as the number of practicing Catholics has shot up, so *santería* is booming too. In few other countries do you see so many young people demonstrating their religiousness by wearing the colourful *santería* necklaces and bracelets or by sporting the all-white uniform demanded of initiates. Some dismiss the revival as a craze, charging that its adherents are attracted not so much by faith as by the music and the street credibility which membership of the faith nowadays seems to endow.

Gods and Divination

Several hundred gods fill the ranks of the Yorubá pantheon, of which only about twenty are consulted regularly. Each is paired up with a Catholic saint according to shared attributes, although the *orisha* or *santo* is generally far more human (and fallible) than its Christian counterpart. For example Ochún, identified with the Catholic Virgin of Charity, the patron saint of Cuba, is the goddess of fresh water and love, but she is represented as a beautiful and flirtatious *mulata*. Dancing is one of Ochún's tools of seduction. In *santería* music forms an integral part of the spiritual experience. On saints' days and other special religious occasions, people celebrate with dancing and singing and, whenever possible, alcohol.

Olofí represents the closest *santería* equivalent to the Catholic supreme god. But the ruler of the Yorubá celestial world would be powerless without Orula, the god of wisdom, who by means of divination allows Olofí and the other *orishas* to communicate with believers. People consult Orula to seek advice before making important decisions. Strong believers may decide to leave the country or get a divorce on the basis of divination.

Santería priests or *babalawos* (the priesthood is male-only) perform divination in their own homes. Various instruments can be used in the process, most commonly the *okpele*, a chain with eight pieces of coconut shell which when swung onto the floor can fall into any of 256 combinations. Each is a sign that carries with it numerous myths and stories amassed over centuries, and which the *babalawo* will interpret for his client.

Sex and Marriage

In a country where everything is either rationed or unobtainable, sex is one of the few aspects of life not controlled by the state. Yet even sex is not without its problems. Housing conditions are so cramped, often with three generations living in one apartment, that couples find it hard to enjoy much privacy. Those with money to spare sometimes resort to spartan "love hotels" called *posadas*, but these grim places rule out any glimmer of romance.

By actively encouraging matrimony and by promoting the concept of the family and offering material incentives to those who tie the knot, the Cuban government has succeeded in more than doubling the annual number of marriages since the Revolution. Even so, and in sharp contrast with other Latin American countries bound by Catholic morality, more than 60 percent of Cuban babies are born out of wedlock. This also reflects the reluctance to use contraception and the high rate of teenage pregnancies; abortion, which has been free and legal since 1965, is the most common method of birth control. In 1995, the rate of abortions per births was a staggering 54.4 per 100 births, although this was a drop on previous years.

Cubans tend to change partners frequently, a habit reflected in the fact that among Cubans aged 25-40, 60 percent of marriages end in divorce. According to official statistics, there was one divorce for every nineteen marriages in 1953; by the 1990s, that figure had risen to roughly one divorce for every two marriages. The government has made getting a divorce cheap and easy, and the trauma of the experience rarely seems to put Cubans off remarrying. Among the reasons for the high divorce rate are the pressures on relationships caused by overcrowding in the home, the decline in the influence of the Catholic Church, and also the changing role of women.

Women

The communist regime has markedly improved women's access to jobs. Having made up less than one-fifth of the workforce before the Revolution, women now represent 40 percent. Women have also broken into traditionally male-dominated spheres such as education and medicine (48 percent of doctors are now women), although they have had less success at entering the upper echelons in any sphere; just a handful of the 24 members of the Party's Politburo are women.

The Cuban Women's Federation (FMC) has helped formulate some remarkably progressive legislation, in particular, the Family Code passed in 1974, which set out the responsibilities of married couples and gave men and women both equal rights and responsibilities for child-rearing, education, and even housework. Such a law cannot be enforced easily, however, and no amount of legislation can crack the *machismo* inherent in Cuban society. Most Cuban families still celebrate a daughter's fifteenth birthday in lavish style to announce her passage to womanhood and, traditionally, her readiness for marriage. And so many women have children before they are twenty that they lose out on the career opportunities that the Revolution opened up for them.

While it is still the case that most men believe it is acceptable for husbands, but not for wives, to be unfaithful, the rise in the divorce rate springs partly from the fact that since the Revolution women now feel more confident about putting an end to unhappy relationships. Equally, some men have found it hard to adjust to the fact that many women now want to work, and have divorced them for supposedly abandoning the home and the household chores. In fact, women still hold the home together and have had to work extremely hard at doing so during the economic crisis.

Homosexuality

Fidel Castro once said that a homosexual could never embody the characteristics of a true revolutionary. Homosexuality was once perceived as the product of decadent, capitalist society, and hundreds of homosexuals were marched off to labor camps to rid them of their supposed moral laxity. Thousands of gay people have left Cuba since the 1960s. Those who have stayed behind and been open about their sexuality have often found their chosen professions closed to them; homosexual teachers, for example, were thought to distort the image of what a good socialist should be.

The issue of homosexuality became a hot topic in the 1990s following the publication in 1989 of *El bosque, el lobo, el hombre nuevo* (The Wood, the Wolf, the New Man), a story by Senel Paz about a sophisticated gay intellectual and his friendship with a straight, young member of the Communist Party. It was the first book in years to deal with homosexuality. The 1993 screen version, *Fresa y chocolate* (Strawberry and Chocolate) ran for months and months in Cuban cinemas. It provoked an unprecedented review of attitudes to homosexuality in Cuba, inspiring numerous articles on the subject in the press.

In 1992, Fidel Castro declared that homosexuality was "a natural human tendency that must simply be respected" and there is definitely more tolerance now. However, reducing homophobia in a society where conventional and heterosexual characteristics have been reinforced by communist morality and the revolutionary ideal of virility cannot be achieved easily. Furthermore, the attitude of the government remains contradictory. Despite Fidel Castro's statements that he is opposed to discrimination against those who are gay, the state provides no publicly gay bars or clubs, and gay men and lesbians still report incidents of official harassment. The law against public displays of homosexuality was abolished in 1987 but this has not put an end to the arrests or fines. Many more people are coming out these days, and a number of gay and lesbian groups are now able to hold meetings, but they are not permitted by law to do so.

On a day-to-day basis, the biggest problem for most gay and lesbian Cubans is the lack of understanding in the family home, and lack of general social acceptance: *maricón*, the local word for gay man, is often used to describe a spineless (heterosexual) man.

Education

José Martí wrote that to be educated is the only way to be free. Cynics might suggest that in Cuba the prime duty of teachers since the Revolution is to turn out well-educated socialists. The education-or-indoctrination debate aside, Castro's regime has replaced a system that provided a decent education only for the rich with one that offers free schooling for everyone and has achieved literacy levels that are the envy of developing countries, and some wealthy capitalist countries as well, around the world.

At the United Nations in 1960, Castro stated that he proposed to eliminate illiteracy in Cuba. Not long afterwards, he dispatched more than 250,000 teachers and schoolchildren into the Cuban interior to teach the peasants to read and write. In a staggering feat of voluntary fervor, illiteracy was reduced from 23.6 percent to 3.9 percent by the end of 1962, providing a benchmark for the regime's achievements.

The slogan "Every worker a student, every student a worker" encapsulates the other main thrust in Castro's educational vision. This ideal prompted the introduction in 1971 of one of the world's most daring experiments in education: the "School in the Country," where students split their time between classes and agricultural work. The Cuban leader's obsession with science has arguably been detrimental to the study of arts subjects, but the number of universities has rocketed, from a paltry three in 1959 to an impressive 40 today.

The economic crisis has put severe pressure on the education system. Teachers are one of the worst paid groups in Cuba, and the stress levels of the job have only intensified during the Special Period. The island's low illiteracy levels are threatened and attendance is seriously disrupted by the shortage of public transport.

Healthcare

The achievements of the Revolution in the field of healthcare have reached almost legendary status. Cuba has created not only a medical service accessible to the entire population, free of charge, but probably the most extensive health system in Latin America.

Before 1959, healthcare was advanced, but few had access to it: 60 percent of Cuba's 6,000 doctors worked in the capital, and half of them left after the Revolution. From such inauspicious beginnings, Cuba now has a vast army of doctors (the highest proportion of doctors per head in Latin America) and a network of polyclinics that extends into every corner of the island. The country's infant mortality rates, which had fallen from 60 deaths per 1,000 in 1958 to 7.1 by 1997, put Cuba in a league with developed countries and above parts of the U.S. Average life expectancy in Cuba is 76 years, compared with a Third World average closer to 57.

The main causes of death in Cuba (cancer, strokes, and heart disease) are equally uncharacteristic of a developing nation. Vaccination drives over the last 30 years have eradicated malaria, polio, and tetanus, and have greatly reduced the incidence of other diseases from tuberculosis to meningitis. Advanced medical science has developed to the point where organ transplants and laser treatment are commonplace. Cuba has managed to build up a significant "health tourism" industry, and over 5,000 people travel to Cuba every year from abroad for specialist medical care. Several hundred Chernobyl children are still on the island undergoing treatment against radiation unavailable to them at home, and victims of the 1997 volcanic eruptions on Montserrat were also treated on the island.

The Cuban government has struggled to maintain its healthcare system since 1989. The flagship Hermanos Almeijeiras Hospital in Havana is kept in reasonable shape, but elsewhere stories of dirty syringes and sticky tape used in the absence of suture material reverberate around the wards. The calorie intake of the average Cuban has dropped by a third making them more likely to succumb to illness.

Medical aid from abroad has been vital in ensuring the supply of at least essential medicines and helping to counter the effects of the U.S. embargo, which denies Cuba access to over 50 percent of the new medicines on the market. Outside the hospitals, most medicines in Cuba are sold in hard currency shops, out of reach of the majority of Cubans. Local people must rely instead on local pharmacies, which look more like museums than dispensing chemists. Here, herbal remedies, which have been developed locally in response to the lack of conventional medicines, are virtually all that are available.

AIDS

In line with its remarkable record in other spheres of healthcare, the number of people infected with HIV and AIDS in Cuba is low compared with other countries in Latin America and the Caribbean, not least its closest neighbor, Haiti. According to official statistics at the end of 1997, there were 1,800 carriers of the HIV virus, 666 people with AIDS (the accumulated total); and 478 had died of AIDS.

Cuba's methods to prevent the spread of AIDS (*SIDA* in Spanish) have caused considerable controversy over the last decade. This has arisen because of the government's introduction of compulsory AIDS tests for adults and the use of sanatoria, where anyone infected with the virus is isolated from the community. Protestors, mostly from abroad, claim that such a policy is a violation of human rights. The Cuban government believes instead that by isolating patients it is defending the rights of the millions of Cubans who are not infected. In the last several years, the government has in fact encouraged a less restrictive regime in the sanatoria. AIDS patients considered fit and sexually responsible are allowed to go out to work and spend more time with their families. Ironically, many patients prefer to stay in the sanatoria because the living conditions and food rations are often better than in their own homes; furthermore, AIDS patients find greater tolerance on the inside.

In Cuba, as elsewhere, AIDS was first dismissed as a gay disease, but half the infections are among heterosexuals. In 98 percent of cases, the virus is transmitted through sex. Education campaigns have concentrated on promoting the use of condoms, but still less than ten percent of Cubans use what is known locally as *el quitasensaciones*, "the killjoy." AIDS remains just a remote danger to the average Cuban.

Domino players, Old Havana

M. O'Brien/Panos

Living with Tourism

The government which abolished Christmas as a public holiday after the Revolution now decks out its hotels in reindeer, snowmen and fairy lights and holds special parties for tourists on 25 December. It seems that as far as tourism is concerned, in Cuba anything goes. Having condemned tourism as the epitome of pre-1959 decadence and inequalities, the government has embraced the industry like a long-lost lover.

Fidel Castro defends such an ideological turnaround with statements about economic necessity, but it is harder for him to justify the exclusion of Cubans from many services offered to foreign visitors. There is the uncomfortable sense that life has gone full circle. As in the Batista days, Cubans find that the island's best beaches, hotels and restaurants are effectively out of bounds. When Cubans go on holiday in the summer, they usually have to stay in very basic peso hotels, while foreign tourists can enjoy the comfort of modernized dollar establishments. The official line is that if local people were allowed to stay in tourist hotels, paying in pesos, there would be less room for foreigners and therefore less hard currency to buy food and other things for the Cuban people. In Castro's own words, "Only a petit bourgeois dandy is unable to understand why Cubans can't use these hotel rooms". The sacrifice must be borne for the sake of socialism.

While everyone appreciates the need for hard currency and sacrifice, many Cubans can't help but resent the tourist apartheid which makes them feel like second-class citizens in their own country. A tourist who is robbed receives more attention from the police than a Cuban; the dollar restaurants serve ingredients that are out of reach of the average Cuban; and a typical night out for most locals is a stroll around the streets, while tourists can drink into the early hours in comfortable hotel bars.

Cubans of all descriptions seek out tourists: some are simply looking for friendship, others, known as *jineteros*, want their money. Male *jineteros* may approach tourists in the street offering cigars or CDs, but Cuba is better known for its female *jineteras*, who seek out single men and will exchange sexual favors sometimes simply for a few free meals and gifts; others may dream of marriage and an easy escape from a hard life in Cuba. As Cuba's economic situation has worsened, more and more women have turned to this kind of prostitution. The regime, which initially dismissed the *jineteras*, as "morally sick" amateurs doing it for clothes rather than real necessities, did little to stop *jineterismo* in the early days, and laid itself open to accusations that it was tolerating sex tourism – already a boom industry in Havana and some of the beach resorts. Nowadays, however, the government has tried to keep tighter control on Cubans entering hotels and resorts in an attempt to deal with the problem – with only limited success.

Havana's "Palestinians"

In 1997, the news spread through the streets of Havana that the government was trying to force tens of thousands of Cubans from Oriente back home. This came after announcements that a new law gave the authorities the power to fine and expel any Cuban not formally registered to live in the capital, and that any Cubans wanting to move to Havana must seek permission to do so.

Such a dramatic move was a response to the sharp rise in the number of "internal migrants" moving to Havana from the eastern provinces. Following an average rate of migration to the capital of 11,000 people per year since the Revolution, during the Special Period this figure shot up to nearer 30,000. It is suggested that there are now as many as 400,000 migrants living in the city. The migrants are known locally as *Palestinos*, an allusion to the fact that they have no "homeland" of their own. It also plays on the fact that many of the migrants live in squatter settlements reminiscent of places like Gaza Strip. With open sewers and no running water, these *barrios* are in danger of turning into the kind of shanty towns that have long afflicted cities elsewhere in Latin America.

In a speech in April 1997, Fidel Castro blamed the migrants for the serious "social indiscipline" in Havana. According to the Communist Party leader in Havana, Esteban Lazo, the migration was also "negating the efforts of the Revolution" in the countryside — a reference to the improvements in housing, education, and healthcare in rural areas since 1959. For many, Havana simply presents better job opportunities, greater access to dollars (via tourism), and also higher food rations.

Crime

Street children do not exist in Cuba, drug addiction is only a small problem, and violent crimes such as rape are rare. But Cuba's relatively crime-free society has been undermined by economic crisis, tourism, and frustration. The majority of Cubans break the law every day simply to survive, by buying food and other necessities on the black market. Beggars, a rarity just five years ago, are now commonplace in Havana: they range from primary school children (sometimes dispatched by their parents to cadge a few coins from tourists) to housewives and pensioners.

The opening of new shops catering for Cubans and tourists with dollars makes people increasingly consumer-conscious and unsympathetic towards the government's calls for sacrifice. The number of bag-snatchings from foreigners is rising and the police presence in tourist centers has been stepped up considerably. The contentious exclusion of local people from some tourist hotels and restaurants, which is most noticeable in Havana, is defended by the establishments as a necessary measure to protect topurists from potential criminals.

The police can do little about bicycle theft, however, which is the most common crime against impoverished Cubans. People who cycle at night risk being ambushed, so now some ride with a machete strapped to their crossbar.

Visitors to the island should bear in mind that the rise in crime began from an extraordinarily low base. Many Westerners find that Cuba is by far the safest country they have ever visited. More Cubans commit crimes against government economic restrictions than against tourists or each other.

6   CULTURE: CARIBBEAN FUSION

"Here everything is resolved with drums and beer"
— *La Bella de la Alhambra*

Cuba has a remarkably rich culture for a country its size — the result of a cross-fertilization of a whole variety of influences, whose flavors have blended to form a delicious and sometimes surprising stew. The French, the Chinese, and the Americans have all made their own contributions to Cuban culture, but the predominant influences have emanated from Spain and Africa.

As the ruling power, the Spanish inevitably dominated culture as they did every other aspect of life in Cuba during the colonial period. They brought their own music, dance, and architecture as well as their own language. There was little competition, since they obliterated indigenous culture and subjugated the thousands of Africans that they brought to the island to work on the plantations. Only after the abolition of slavery were Afro-Cubans finally able to express themselves, and help shape and enrich Cuba's essentially European traditions to form the unmistakable culture that is characteristic of the island today.

After independence from Spain, the arts in Cuba blossomed, in the fields of art, literature, architecture, and music. By the time Fidel Castro came to power, Havana was one of the top cultural centers in Latin America. In line with its activities in other fields, the government began state sponsorship of the arts following the Revolution, creating institutions such as the ICAIC (the Cuban Institute of Film Art and Industry). The most beneficial effect of the Revolution's promotion of culture for the masses was the broadening of cultural life to reach the entire Cuban population. Every sizeable town now has its own museum, cultural center, theatre, and cinema, to which access is either free or very cheap.

It also sought to exert control over the world of culture. Intellectuals existed to serve socialism and the masses, not the elite. Cuba lost fine people as some of the best and boldest writers, artists, and musicians chose exile rather than artistic asphyxiation, oblivion, or forced labor. Cuba sank into cultural isolation, cut off from all but Eastern European influences. (Interestingly, despite 30 years' involvement in the island, the USSR had no lasting impact on Cuban culture.)

As early as 1961, Fidel Castro told writers and artists: "Everything within the Revolution, nothing against the Revolution." Cuban artists and intellectuals have learned to work within the parameters set by the government, in many cases storing their work for the post-Castro era. Others have chosen

CUBA

The Cuban flag was first flown by anti-Spanish rebels in 1850 and was adopted when the republic became formally independent in 1902. The three blue stripes stand for the three departments into which Cuba was then divided. The white stripes symbolise the purity of independence, while the red is the blood which was shed to achieve it. The white star is a masonic emblem of independence.

Cuban flag and monument to Antonio Maceo
(Paul Schatzberger/South American Pictures)

The cathedral, old Havana
(Rolando Pujol/South American Pictures)

Havana street life
(Simon Calder)

Any Cuban can identify the names and faces of the country's extensive pantheon of national heroes, from the freedom fighters of the 19th century, such as Manuel Céspedes and Antonio Maceo, to those of the 1959 Revolution, such as Camilio Cienfuegos and Frank País. They are commemorated in the names of streets throughout the island, and in the string of anniversaries that fills the Cuban calendar. The promotion of such figures and dates helps lend legitimacy to the current regime by the sheer weight of history. Fidel Castro claims to be simply carrying on a historical process begun by the first revolutionaries to take up arms last century. He still ends most speeches with the rallying cry used during the War of Independence: 'Fatherland or Death! We will conquer!'.

One name, one face appears above all others. That of José Martí. The inspiration for the War of Independence, he has remained the standard bearer of Cubans' aspirations for change throughout the 20th century, and Fidel Castro still regularly invokes his ideas. The mass-produced bust of Martí decorates small secular shrines all over the island.

May Day celebrations in Plaza de la Revolución, Havana
(Julio Etchart/Reportage)

'Always heroic', Santiago
(M. O' Brien/Panos)

Cuba's pantheon of national heroes
(Julio Etchart/Reportage)

Che Guevara, the ultimate revolutionary icon
(Osvaldo Salas/Reportage)

The only other man honoured with a place in Havana's Plaza de la Revolución, alongside Martí, is Che Guevara. Despite abandoning most of Che's ideas, the Cuban regime continues to play on his popularity, both at home and abroad, as the world's archetypal romantic hero – though his well-known image is used more than his words.

Other great symbols of Cuba – cigars and rum cocktails – rose to worldwide fame before 1959. Even the Tropicana cabaret, the symbol of the decadence under Batista, has survived almost four decades of communism. But, like rum and tobacco, it is enjoyed more by tourists than by Cubans.

The Tropicana nighclub
(M. O' Brien/Panos)

Hemingway haunt – La Floridita, Havana
(M. O' Brien/Panos)

Granma, the national paper, *a mojito*, the national drink
(Simon Tang)

Vintage US car outside Capitol in Havana
(Julio Etchart/Reportage)

to collaborate to improve their chance of a successful career; international recognition is virtually impossible without official backing.

The Special Period has brought both benefits and hardships. The shortages of money and materials have adversely affected all fields of cultural life. Publishing output has been affected, while performances in theaters and cinemas have been reduced to a minimum. The rise in tourism and in foreign investment has brought much needed resources into these same areas, but the reality is that the majority of books published, CDs made, concerts laid on, and paintings exhibited are available only to those with dollars to spend. A cultural evening for most Cubans is a night in front of the television, where educational programs are interlaced with music videos, pirated movies from North America, and Brazilian soaps.

Music

Cuba has one of the world's richest and most original musical traditions. Music is not just a passion, but an intrinsic part of the Cuban temperament.

Cuban music was extremely influential internationally in the decades running up to the Revolution. After 1959, some musicians left, while others had to come to terms with the island's international isolation. In the last decade Cuba has found itself back on the world scene. While this success has been due largely to the boom in salsa music, traditional rhythms and jazz have also found an international audience.

Many of the island's top groups spend substantial amounts of time abroad, either recording or touring. Back home, the opportunities for both are extremely limited. There is just one record company, EGREM, which is always short of resources. Professional musicians are employed by the government, and state evaluating committees keep tight control over the kind of music played. Some groups that have been performing for twenty years have never been allowed to record an album.

Fernando Ortíz, the first person to undertake serious research into Afro-Cuban culture, in the early twentieth century, wrote that most of the island's music sprang from "the love affair of African drums and Spanish guitar." It was only with the absorption of Afro-Cubans into society following the abolition of slavery that music really took off in Cuba. The white middle classes were almost schizophrenic in their musical tastes in the early twentieth century, fascinated by the intoxicating rhythms produced by their black compatriots, yet resistant to abandoning their more sedate dances.

Son, which hit Havana in around 1910, was the most significant early manifestation of the fusion of Hispanic and African music. It developed among the ballad (*trova*) singers of eastern Cuba, who added African drums to the traditional accompaniment of just a guitar. Small groups soon developed into full-blown orchestras, with a double bass, trumpets, and a whole range of percussion instruments. The Septeto Nacional of Ignacio Piñeiro was one of the first

Salsa rhythms in Havana

Rolando Pujol/South American Pictures

orchestras to make *son* famous in the 1920s. Two decades later Beny Moré, nicknamed *El Bárbaro del Ritmo*, "The Wild Man of Rhythm," became a legend in his own time as Cuba's best-loved *son* artist.

Son has inspired Cuban musicians ever since, and is considered the most influential genre in Latin American music. Traditional *son* is of enduring popularity in Cuba, but it has also spawned numerous variations, from *mambo* and *cha-cha-chá*, which swept the world in the 1940s and 1950s, to salsa. The latter emerged in New York in the 1970s as a combination of all kinds of Latin rhythms, but few would dispute its origins in Cuban *son*. In Cuba, the salsa movement really picked up steam in the late 1980s and early 1990s, and now dominates the music scene in the island. Critics dismiss Cuban salsa as vulgar, superficial, and over-simplistic, but as Issac Delgado, one of Cuba's leading *salseros* once said "Popular dance music... is for dancing. People don't go to a dance to think."

Salsa has evolved dramatically in Cuba, so that it is no longer simply *son* but a combination of Cuban and international rhythms that some refer to as *timba* or Cuban funk. Bands like NG La Banda, La Charanga Habanera, and Issac Delgado lead the field in this style of salsa and have a fanatical following, not just for the music but for the streetwise lyrics that express better than anything else young people's hopes and fears. Longer-standing orchestras have also been given a new lease of life by the salsa boom. Los Van Van, led by Juan Formell and performing for some 30 years, is still often considered as the best dance band in Cuba.

There is a strong jazz tradition in Cuba too. The intoxicating blend of jazz and Latin popular rhythms that is characteristic of Cuban jazz was the result of a collaboration between American and Cuban musicians in the 1940s, when men like Mario Bauzá and Chano Pozo worked with greats like Dizzy

Gillespie. Irakere, the best known exponents of Cuban jazz, enrich their music with Afro-Cuban rhythms.

Most music on the island could be described as Afro-Cuban — African rhythms and songs have become the basis for much of the country's jazz and popular music — but the term is normally used to describe only the purest forms of black music. These sound more like the authentic rhythms of Africa than those of a Latin American disco.

Rumba, the most accessible Afro-Cuban music, has been around since the end of the nineteenth century. It first emerged among urban blacks, mostly in Havana and nearby Matanzas, where it absorbed influences from African religious music. One of the most famous *rumba* dances, the *columbia*, is a fast and almost acrobatic solo man's dance based on the moves of the devils that feature in certain ceremonies of the Afro-Cuban cult of Abakuá. The dominant rhythm of *rumba* is played out on tall hand drums known as *congas*.

African rhythms remain in their most unadulterated form in Yorubá ritual music. Complex and intoxicating rhythms designed to invoke the gods are played out on hourglass-shaped drums called *batás*, which are themselves revered as religious objects. They are accompanied by a soloist and chorus singing songs of praise (known as *cantos*) and dancing. The Havana-based Conjunto Nacional Folklórico (the National Folklore Group) has helped to popularize Yorubá music.

Cuba's carnivals, which originated in colonial times to allow slaves to celebrate the end of the sugar harvest or *zafra*, are the most vibrant expression of Afro-Cuban music and dance. Held at the end of July, they revolve around processions known as *comparsas*. The carnival in Santiago de Cuba, the most famous in the island, is one of the best cultural events in Latin America.

Youth Music

You won't often find *roqueros, freakies,* or *metálicos* dancing salsa. Rockers, hippies, and heavy metal fans (respectively) prefer to grow their hair long and sway to American rock. Once upon a time, jeans and long hair were considered symbols of "ideological deviance" and listening to the Beatles or Santana a gesture of protest.

Not surprisingly, such prejudice did not encourage much of a home-grown rock movement. After the Revolution, politically-minded musicians breathed life into the old ballad tradition and created *nueva trova,* the only significant musical movement to have emerged since 1959. Silvio Rodríguez and Pablo Milanés, its main exponents, did not go down well with the regime initially. Milanés, known for his outspoken lyrics, even spent time in a labor camp. Both have since made their peace with the authorities and are now strongly supported by the regime. They perform regularly, both at home and abroad, and are viewed as key international symbols of the Revolution.

The younger generation of *nueva trova* performers are more influenced by rock than their predecessors. In the 1980s, the role of protest singer was taken up by Carlos Varela. With his beard and black hat, he veers more towards folk than rock, but he voices the frustrations of some young Cubans, above all their desire for change. Varela's music was banned for a time, but since he has never called for violent protest some radio stations now give him airtime, and he has shared a stage with Castro himself.

The acceptance of Varela and other exponents of rock has coincided with a general cultural opening since the late 1980s, which has improved access to international music and led to a greater tolerance of rock. But while rock music features on Cuban television and radio (there is even a national rock festival), few bands have made it into a recording studio. And despite greater acceptance on the part of the authorities, many Cubans remain prejudiced against such music and its fans, who are still perceived as being by definition rebellious.

Ballet

As far as traditional performing arts are concerned, Cuba is best known for its ballet. The Ballet Nacional de Cuba, founded in 1948, has an established reputation at home and abroad for its performances of both modern and classical work. Its success is largely thanks to the work of its founder, prima ballerina Alicia Alonso, who enjoys the affectionate title "First Lady of Cuba." Links with the Kirov and Bolshoi ballet companies of the Soviet Union since the 1960s have also been beneficial. The Ballet of Camagüey, founded after the Revolution and directed for many years by Fernando Alonso (the husband of Alicia), is Cuba's best provincial ballet company, but it struggles to keep hold of its top dancers, who are drawn either to Havana or overseas.

Film

The Cuban regime has devoted more attention to film than to any other art form since the revolution. For many years, film was seen primarily as a tool of political education. The Cuban Institute of Film Art and Industry (ICAIC) was founded in the first year of the revolution to make documentaries that would promote the policies of the regime. Traveling projection units were sent to all corners of the island, spreading the word amongst the people. This kind of propaganda film became a model for similar films all over Latin America.

While documentaries still represent the bulk of the industry's output, feature films arouse most interest, both at home and abroad. Cubans adore the movies and will line up for hours to see a new release. Despite the shadow cast by ICAIC, directors have managed to retain some autonomy and tackle important social issues head on. A series of talented directors, such as Humberto Solás and Tomás Gutiérrez Alea, are among the most creative artists to have worked successfully under the Revolution. Alea, known for classics such as *Memorias del subdesarrollo* (Memories of Underdevelopment, 1969) and *La Muerte de un burócrata* (Death of a Bureaucrat, 1966) shot back to fame in the 1990s with *Fresa y chocolate* (Strawberry and Chocolate). This film was promoted more than any other film in recent memory, its frank treatment of the problems in Cuban society being described in the official Cuban press as "constructive criticism." The film won an award at the Berlin Film Festival in 1994 and an Oscar nomination in 1995 for Best Foreign Film.

Such awards are received gladly. Cinema is important for Cuba's prestige abroad, culturally and politically, as well as a source of hard currency. It is significant that Cuba has not sacrificed the annual New Latin American Film Festival, established in 1979, to the Special Period. It draws a large international audience and provides a springboard for the release of Cuban films made in increasingly difficult conditions. The Coral prizes awarded at the festival are considered Latin America's equivalent of the Oscars.

Restored street in Old Havana

Rolando Pujol/South American Pictures

Havana Style

Old *Habaneros* remember their city as the grandest and most beautiful in Latin America. Looking down on central Havana's rooftops now, you would be forgiven for thinking you had landed in war-ravaged Sarajevo. The city is not just peeling at the edges, but crumbling and falling apart. The preservation of old architecture never featured on the list of Marxist priorities. Indeed, following the Revolution, the policy was consciously to neglect the capital given that it had received earlier governments' undivided attention for years, to the detriment of the rest of the country.

In 1982, most of central Havana was added to UNESCO's list of World Heritage Sites. Restorers are now working feverishly to make up for lost time. They have already restored the cream of the capital's early buildings, which rub shoulders with overcrowded and decrepit tenement blocks along the narrow streets of Old Havana. The unmistakable look of the city's colonial buildings, with their solid, tropical grace, derives from the fusion of the *mudéjar* style, the blend of Christian and Muslim traditions brought by craftsman from Andalucía in Spain, with more sophisticated baroque influences. The eighteenth-century house of Conde de Casa Bayona, in Cathedral Square, is a typical *Habanero* colonial home. The central courtyard is enclosed by an arcaded gallery, with walls painted yellow and wooden balustrades icy blue: a sea-and-sand color combination which recurs all over Old Havana. Upstairs, the *mudéjar* carpenters made some of the city's finest ceilings, the so-called *alfarjes*. Geometric star patterns decorate the beams — an Islamic representation of the universe that the Christian residents did not seem to mind.

Literature

The Argentinian journalist, Jacobo Timerman, wrote that "If it is true that every Cuban knows how to read and write, it is likewise true that every Cuban has nothing to read and must be very cautious about what he writes." In most Cuban bookstores, the complete works of Lenin gather dust on half-empty shelves alongside dreary tomes about crop management and Marxist theory.

Many of Cuba's most acclaimed writers of the nineteenth and twentieth centuries spent their formative years in exile. The greatest novelist of the last century, Cirilo Villaverde (1812-44) was an open opponent of Spanish colonial rule and spent many years in exile in the United States. His most famous work, a love story called *Cecilia Valdés*, published in 1838, is strongly evocative of the struggles endured by slaves during Spanish rule. The works of José Martí, who also spent years in Spain and the U.S., fill several feet of shelf space in most bookshops. He was a poet as well as a journalist and political activist, his *Versos sencillos* being his best known collection of poems.

During the harsh climate of the "pseudo" republic, many Cuban writers chose or were forced to live abroad. Among them was Alejo Carpentier (1904-1980), Cuba's most revered writer of this century. He was imprisoned in the 1920s by the Machado regime and later lived in exile, mainly in Paris. He returned to Cuba after the Revolution, and became the head of the national publishing company as well as a professor at Havana University. An exponent of the Latin American style of writing known as "magic realism," he often used distinctly avant-garde imagery. Among his most famous works are *El Siglo de las luces* (1962; translated as *Explosion in a Cathedral*), a historic novel set in the Caribbean at the time of the French revolution, and *Concierto barroco* (1974), about a journey of mutual discovery by a rich Mexican and his servant.

Cuba's other great twentieth-century writer, Nicolás Guillén (1902-89), also lived abroad during the Batista years. Cuba's National Poet and a lifelong communist, Guillén wrote many poems in praise of the Revolution's achievements and was a loyal participant in the country's cultural and political life. Of mixed African and Hispanic descent, he used musical rhythms to cut his poetry to a distinct Afro-Cuban mold.

The years immediately after the Revolution witnessed something of a literary boom, but that came to an abrupt halt with the so-called Padilla

Affair in 1968. This involved the arrest of Heberto Padilla after he was given an award (by an international jury) for a collection of poems that was critical of the Revolution. The writer's arrest and the banning of the book by the government prompted an outcry among intellectuals abroad, including those who hitherto had been supportive of the regime. Public letters of protest signed by the likes of Gabriel García Márquez (now a close friend of Fidel Castro) and Jean-Paul Sartre appeared in several newspapers, but to no avail. Strict censorship became the order of the day and many writers left the country, including Guillermo Cabrera Infante, considered Cuba's greatest living author. He lives in London and is a rabid critic of the Cuban regime. Many of his works have been translated into English, including *Tres tristes tigres* (Three Trapped Tigers), set in pre-revolutionary Havana.

Many writers who have matured under the Revolution continue to draw inspiration from Afro-Cuban culture. Miguel Barnet, one of Cuba's most important living authors still living on the island, is one of the island's few modern writers to have an international reputation. His best-known book, *Biografía de un cimarrón*, published in 1967 and later translated as *The Autobiography of a Runaway Slave*, began a small trend for the so-called "testimonial novel," which recounts the life of a living person in the individual's own words. More recently, younger authors such as Senel Paz and the late Reinaldo González have grappled with new and grittier issues ranging from homosexuality and tourism to AIDS.

Art

After the revolution, Fidel Castro rejected the idea of art as an end in itself, declaring instead that "Man is the end." However, he drew back from banning abstract art, as he was encouraged to do by Moscow and by hard-liners in his own ranks. As a result, Cuban artists are able to express themselves more freely than in any other field of the arts. Artists must contend with the inevitable state control of art galleries, but the legalization of self-employment means that many artists are now able to sell their work directly to the public. Nowadays, the main source of frustration for artists is the appalling shortage of materials.

Compared with the largely unremarkable art produced during the colonial period, the work produced during the twentieth century has been rich indeed. Many Cuban painters traveled to Europe during the early decades of the 1900s and were inspired by what was being produced by artists from Gauguin to Chagall. Cuba's most famous artist of this century, Wilfredo Lam (1902–82), spent his formative years in Paris, where he met and worked with Picasso, and was greatly influenced by the surrealist movement. René Portocarrero (1912–85) produced striking paintings using vivid oils and also stained-glass windows.

Baseball is Cuba's number one sport

Julio Etchart/Reportage

The island's most renowned living artists include Manuel Mendive, whose works are inspired by Afro-Cuban mythology and folklore, and Flora Fong, of Sino-Cuban descent, who creates vibrant Caribbean landscapes.

Sport

Cubans need little encouragement to enjoy sport as far as spectating is concerned, but for Fidel Castro participation is crucial. He preaches that sport is a vital part of a person's education — both physical and moral. Sport, Cubans are told, is an antidote to vice.

Whatever people think of their leader's philosophy, Castro's regime has succeeded in raising the country's sporting achievement to unimaginable heights. Before the Revolution, Cubans were known for their success in the boxing ring and on the baseball field, but had only ever won a handful of Olympic gold medals. In 1976, at the Montréal Olympics, Cuba came eighth in the medal table with six golds. Two decades later, in Atlanta, Cuba came eighth again, this time winning nine golds (including four for boxing). In terms of population, this level of success is remarkable.

Sport is a matter of national pride, and despite Cuba's crippled economy, Castro refused to renege on his promise to host the Pan-American Games in 1991. The Villa Pan Americana, built just outside Havana for the tournament, stands as a monument to the leadership's determination to defend the island's international image. The games proved to be a great success since Cuba walked off with 140 gold medals — more than any other nation. It was the first time a Latin American country had ever bettered the U.S.

Success in sports brings material benefits for individuals as well as the kind of prestige and adulation characteristic in other countries. Javier Sotomayor, the world record holder in the high jump, and considered by some to be the greatest high-jumper of all time, is a hero in Cuba. He is also a deputy in the National Assembly. Given the privileges that sportspeople enjoy in Cuba, and given their high profile on the international sporting scene, it is a severe blow to the regime when athletes decide to defect. The Atlanta games in 1996, which saw defections by three Cuban competitors, was no exception.

It is baseball, or *pelota*, that arouses the greatest passions in Cuba. Kids play it in the street from the moment they can walk. Adults argue about it every day under the trees in Havana's Parque Central. Men and women together scream and shout from the terraces during matches, and the country grinds to a halt during the climax of the National Series. This usually involves two of the big four teams: Industriales (of Havana), Santiago, Pinar del Río, and Villa Clara.

The Americans brought baseball to Cuba in the 1860s. It caught on so quickly that by 1872 Havana had founded its own baseball club. The Spanish banned it at first, on the pretext that the Cubans used games as a cover for conspiring against them, so the sport failed to develop seriously until after independence. By the 1940s, the Cuban baseball team was often champion of the World Amateur Series, and the country's top players infiltrated major league baseball in the U.S. Fidel Castro himself was perhaps Cuba's top pitcher at that time, and had he not chosen to get involved in politics, he probably would have been pitching for the Washington Senators or the New York Giants.

Cuban players have lost none of their panache under communism and generally compete well at the international level; the Cuban team breezed through the baseball competition at Atlanta to win gold. Many of its top players are being eyed enviously by U.S. teams, anxious to attract them to the professional game. For some the temptation of U.S. salaries is too great. Livan Hernández, one of Cuba's top players, defected in 1995 and signed up with the Florida Marlins for an estimated $4 million. The team went on to win the World Series in 1997, and Hernández himself won the title Most Valuable Player.

CONCLUSION

The revolutionaries have moved out of the Habana Libre Hotel, which is now in the hands of a Spanish tourism company. Security guards keep a close eye on who goes in and out. Most Cubans are turned away. Inside, tourists enjoy a coke and a ham and cheese sandwich, paid for in dollars and costing the equivalent of two weeks' pay for the average Cuban. Across the street, *Habaneros* wait for hours at the state-run Coppelia ice cream parlor, where they pay for a cone in pesos. Is this what the Cuban Revolution was fought for?

In 1959, amidst the euphoria which followed the arrival of the idealistic young revolutionaries to power, people called their offspring Libertad and Fidel in honor of the Revolution. Some Cubans still worship their leader as a hero, but many dismiss him (and the regime over which he presides) as an anachronism. Everyone, from hard-liners to quasi-liberals, wishes to protect the improvements in welfare achieved since 1959, but the contradictions that have arisen out of Cuba's current system are only too obvious. The island boasts some of the best health indicators of any developing country, yet it cannot feed its people. It has free hospitals and a whole army of doctors, yet people cannot buy aspirin unless they have dollars. "Why is the Pope coming to Cuba?" ran a joke in 1998. "Because he wants to see hell first-hand."

In 1997, billboards appeared in Cuba proclaiming: "There will be no transition." The example of the former Eastern bloc, where the move from socialism to free-market economics and multi-party democracy resulted in a serious fall in living standards and huge social problems, has undoubtedly influenced the decision by the Cuban leadership to slow its reform program. But the very concept of transition seems to be anathema to the regime. Any hint that the Cuban experiment has failed, or that the regime has given in to pressure from the U.S., is simply inconceivable.

Ever since reforms were first introduced in Cuba, outsiders have wondered how far down the route of free-market economics the regime would go. Castro's government may have already gone as far as it intends to. By 1998 virtually all of Cuba's provincial party leaders and many Central Committee members outside of Havana were of the new generation — in their late 30s and 40s. They do not seem to support farther-reaching market reforms than their older colleagues. There is a good chance that cries of *Socialismo o Muerte!* will see the Cubans into the third millenium.

The continued presence of Fidel Castro is the greatest influence on the future of Cuba, but the role of the U.S. cannot be underestimated. Only the embargo separates the island from an invasion of Dunkin' Donuts, tourists, and, according to recent research, hordes of pensioners in search of a quiet

Sign of the times, a vintage removals van, Havana   (Rolando Pujol/South American Pictures)

spot to spend their retirement. In 1997, Castro made an off-hand suggestion that Bill Clinton should visit Havana. There are few American presidents who would have the political courage to accept such an invitation.

Roberto Robaina once said "We don't need another Fidel," but his will be a hard act to follow. The world will be watching closely.

WHERE TO GO, WHAT TO SEE

A couple of decades ago, most foreign visitors to Cuba were either Eastern Europeans enjoying a reward in the sun for hard work in their cold homelands, or communist sympathizers who visited as part of international brigades to help out with construction work or the harvest. While tourists nowadays are a more conventional bunch, drawn by the increasingly well-advertised classic Caribbean offerings of tropical beaches, colonial architecture, and relaxed, vacation-in-the-sun lifestyle, Cuba has much more to offer than the average Caribbean destination — whether you are into music, old cars, cigars, or socialist regimes struggling against the odds in a capitalism-dominated world.

Cuba has superb colonial architecture — most famously in Old Havana and Trinidad, both of which have been designated as World Heritage Sites by UNESCO, and have enjoyed much attention from restorers. Other large towns, such as Camagüey and Santiago de Cuba, also boast important colonial buildings, but more charming are backwaters like Remedios and Gibara, which are visited by comparatively few tourists and have a more appealing atmosphere of faded grandeur.

While pictures of colonial treasures feature in most tourist brochures, it is the island's beaches that are pushed as the main attraction. While they are not the best in the Caribbean, Cuba has some good beaches — particularly those along the north coast, where the island's most important resorts are located, both on the mainland and on offshore keys: Varadero, within easy reach of Havana; the islands of Cayo Coco and Cayo Guillermo; and Guardalavaca in Oriente. As elsewhere in the Caribbean, the beaches tend to be narrow, but the sand is fine, snowy white and the sea generally clean and clear. The best beaches are given over to resorts devoted to package tourism, although on the small island of Cayo Levisa, off the north coast of Pinar del Río province, simple accommodation in cabins appeals to independent travelers after peace and quiet. In any of the above places, you'll have few Cubans for company. If you want to see Cubans enjoying themselves by the seaside, head for beaches like Guanabo in Playas del Este, east of Havana.

Cuba's beach resorts offer the usual array of water sports, from jet-skiing to windsurfing. The island is also a major diving destination. The string of coral reefs that surrounds much of the Cuban archipelago does not support such an abundance of tropical fish as the waters off the nearby Cayman Islands, but there is a rich variety of sponges and corals, and caves and shipwrecks provide added interest. All the main resorts have diving centers, which offer both trips and training courses, but the most famous dive sites are off the west coast of the Isle of Youth, where the Hotel Colony caters almost exclusively to divers. Santa María La Gorda in Pinar del Río province is another specialist diving center.

Fishing for marlin, swordfish, and other game fish draws sports fishermen to Havana and Varadero in the summer. Ernest Hemingway, who made deep-sea fishing in the Gulf Stream off the north coast of Cuba famous in his novel *The Old Man and the Sea*, has an annual marlin fishing tournament named after him; the competition takes place in May at Tarará Marina, east of Havana.

Cuba has some gorgeous scenery. The island's three mountain ranges are frustratingly hard to explore unless you have an adventurous streak, but the authorities are gradually turning their attention to opening up these wilderness areas. The easiest to explore is the Viñales Valley in western Cuba, on foot or on horseback. The more dramatic Escambray and Sierra Maestra ranges are still most easily appreciated from behind the wheel of a car, although there are now guided treks from Santo Domingo, in the western reaches of the Sierra Maestra, to sites associated with the guerrilla campaign against Batista in the 1950s. The journey between Marea del Portillo and Santiago de Cuba, along a road jammed up against the coast by the southwestern foothills of the Sierra Maestra, is one of the most memorable in the country.

Facilities in Cuba's various protected areas are extremely limited, which leaves much of the island's vaunted abundance of animal and plant species out of reach. The most rewarding area to visit is the Zapata Swamp (Ciénaga de Zapata): go in winter to avoid the worst of the mosquitoes and to catch the migrant birds that migrate from North America for the winter. The area is vast and impenetrable without a guide.

Cuba offers very different experiences depending on how you choose to travel. While a package vacation, whether a stay-put beach holiday, a cultural bus tour, or a combination of the two, may seem an attractive option because the logistics of arranging your own travel and accommodation are taken care of, traveling in a group or staying at a beach resort may stop you experiencing the "real" Cuba.

Anyone travelling independently should not try to cover too much of the island. The size of Cuba (and the length of journeys by road) takes many visitors by surprise. If you have just a couple of weeks, you would be advised to focus on one section of the island rather than trying to do a whistle-stop tour of the whole lot. Since much of the enjoyment revolves around chance encounters with people and the fascination of watching Cubans go about their daily lives, you will miss out if you have an action-packed itinerary. Cuba and haste do not go together.

Despite logistical problems, traveling around Cuba is easy in fun. People are very friendly and eager to help (sometimes too eager). In Havana and the resorts, many people speak English.

Recommended places to visit, beginning with Havana and then running west to east through the island:

Havana: The political and cultural capital of Cuba, with a population of two million, is probably the most exciting city in Latin America. One of *the* places to be seen in the 1950s, Havana is once more one of the trendiest places on the planet. The city is unlike anywhere else on earth, managing to be both seedy and stylish. Havana is irresistible but it is also exhausting. While at least three days are needed to do the city justice, you should line up a quiet couple of days to recuperate afterwards.

There is splendid colonial architecture in Old Havana; the narrow streets of the oldest part of the city, centered around the Plaza de la Catedral and the Plaza de Armas, are choked with tourists in high season, while the nineteenth-century era Parque Central and the Prado (a boulevard reminiscent of the Ramblas in Barcelona), are less precious. In this area, top attractions are the Pártagas cigar factory and the Museo de la Revolución (in Batista's presidential palace), where you will learn everything you ever wanted to know (and more) about the Revolution.

Havana has the best nightlife on the island. A trip to the gaudy Tropicana open-air cabaret is compulsory for some visitors, but serious salsa-lovers are more likely to prefer the Palacio de la Salsa or Casa de la Música. The bars where Ernest Hemingway and other celebrities hung out, such as the plush Floridita and more down-to-earth Bodeguita del Medio, are tourist traps. All these places are beyond the pockets of most Cubans. For a taste of how Habaneros relax on a Saturday night, go and hang out on the Malecón along the seafront.

Viñales Valley: With its landscape of tobacco fields scattered with giant limestone outcrops, the Viñales Valley is one of the most beautiful spots in Cuba. The tranquility of the place and the friendliness of the local people are as seductive as the scenery. There are walks to do, horses to hire, and tobacco farms and caves to visit. Alternatively, you may content yourself with the view from the Hotel Jazmines.

Varadero: This is the largest resort in Cuba, with a string of hotels that increases annually. Claims that the beach at Varadero is the best in the Caribbean are misplaced, but the twelve-mile beach is superb and the facilities good. It is possible to make forays to Cuban towns nearby, such as Matanzas, or to take trips further afield, but few people seem to bother. Curiously, the unpleasant sulfurous smells that emanate from nearby oil wells do not get a mention in the tourist brochures.

Isle of Youth (*Isla de la Juventud*): The island doesn't have much to offer unless you like exploring backwaters. You can visit the prison where Fidel

Castro was held following the attack on the Moncada barracks in 1953, but otherwise the main attraction is the diving off the west coast near Hotel Colony.

Cayo Largo: East of the Isla de la Juventud, and measuring just 25 miles long and up to five miles wide, Cayo Largo is devoted exclusively to tourism. Playa Sirena is one of Cuba's best beaches, but why go all the way to Cuba only to end up stuck on an island with no chance to explore further afield?

Playa Girón: The failed Bay of Pigs invasion of 1961 is commemorated at Playa Girón, on the south coast of the Zapata Swamp. A museum here gives a good description of Cuba's version of the story. You can dive directly from the shore, and from nearby Playa Larga you can arrange guided nature walks into the Zapata Swamp.

Trinidad: The best-preserved colonial town in Cuba, in the shadow of the Escambray mountains, Trinidad was not even linked by road to the rest of the country until the 1950s. Nowadays, it is little more than a living museum — at least in the daytime. To best enjoy Trinidad, stroll through the cobbled streets after the tourist buses have departed. There is a pleasant beach a few miles away, overlooked by two large hotels.

Santa Clara: A buzzing provincial town, with a pleasant Parque Central, Santa Clara is most famous for its connection with Che Guevara, whose attack on a Batista troop train in the city in December 1958 helped persuade the dictator that his days were numbered. The remains of the armored train are now a museum, and you can also visit the resting place of Che himself: following their discovery in Bolivia, the revolutionary's remains were brought to Santa Clara in December 1997 and placed inside the Che monument on the edge of the city.

Remedios: A small community near Santa Clara, Remedios was one of Cuba's most important towns in the colonial era. With most of the buildings in need of a lick of paint, nowadays it is the epitome of faded grandeur. There is a magnificent church in the main square, and a quirky collection of museums. The nation's most exciting festival after the Santiago carnival — a riot of fireworks, music, and parades — takes place on the last Saturday of the year.

Cayo Coco and Cayo Guillermo: These islands off the north coast, both with gorgeous beaches, are being developed exclusively for tourism and already have several luxury hotels. While there is not much in the way of entertainment, at least these islands (unlike Cayo Largo) are within easy reach of the mainland — to which they are linked by a causeway.

Playa Santa Lucía: This is one of the north coast's smaller resorts. It is fairly isolated, lying north of the city of Camagüey. The beach in the resort proper is not Cuba's best, but Playa Los Cocos, a few miles away, certainly is.

Camagüey: One of Cuba's most important cities in the colonial period, Camagüey has a wealth of fine baroque churches and some picturesque nooks and crannies, such as the restored Plaza San Juan de Dios. Perhaps due to its location among the plains of central Cuba, the city sees comparatively few tourists. As a result, Camagüey is a good example of a living, breathing Cuban city.

Guardalavaca: The largest resort in eastern Cuba is in a more scenic spot than its counterparts elsewhere on the island. The beach is pleasant, and nearby Playa Esmeralda is even better. Within easy reach are the delightful town of Gibara, an Indian burial ground (Chorro de Maita), and Bahía de Bariay, where Columbus first set foot on land in Cuba in 1492.

Santiago de Cuba: Cuba's second city is hot, hilly, and exhausting. Its most famous sight is the Moncada barracks, now a museum. Other attractions are the Casa de Velazquez (claimed to be the oldest house in the Americas) in the main square, the cemetery where José Martí and other Cuban heroes are buried, and the famous Casa de la Trova, where local musicians gather and perform daily. Santiago also has its own version of Havana's kitsch Tropicana cabaret.

Guantánamo: The town of Guantánamo has few obvious attractions, but at the Guantánamo Hotel you can arrange a trip to a look-out point (Los Malones) inside the nearby Cuban military zone, for a view over the U.S. Naval Base.

Baracoa: This remote, sleepy port, set among cocoa and coconut groves on the far eastern shores of Cuba, lies at the end of a stunning drive over the Sierra Maestra. It is the oldest town not just in Cuba but in the Americas. Baracoa should be enjoyed at a gentle pace, but there are rivers and mountains to explore, and some good beaches.

TIPS FOR TRAVELERS

When to Go

The best time to visit Cuba is between November and April, the island's (comparatively) cool and dry season. Temperatures are warm (averaging 80°F) but not unbearably hot and humid — as they can be in summer, when the average temperature is 90°F. Visitors who go in summer hoping to do serious sightseeing usually end up doing what most Cubans do, i.e., spending as much time as they can by the sea or in the shower. The summer is also the season for thunderstorms and hurricanes, June and October generally being the wettest months. Be warned that temperatures are even higher in eastern Cuba, particularly in Santiago, which is surrounded by mountains. The high season as far as airfares and hotel costs are concerned is December to January and July to August.

Getting Around

The most popular package holidays to Cuba come in the form of a stay-put beach vacation. Cultural bus tours are also popular and take the headache out of organizing transport and accommodation. But while tourism is geared towards package vacationers, there are no restrictions placed on independent travel. And only by traveling independently are you likely to get the full taste of Cuba.

There are trains between Cuba's main towns, but the only dependable service is between Havana and Santiago. Buses are packed and services infrequent. Organized day trips are a good option if you are staying by the beach and want to make just a couple of forays outside the resort. Those with the time and the inclination should try hitchhiking: since the onset of the Special Period, state-owned vehicles are obliged to pick people up from official hitching points.

The best way to travel long distances if you have limited time is to take internal flights, which are cheap and reasonably reliable and frequent. Generally, however, the best way to get around is to rent a car. Outside the cities there is minimal traffic on the road, and you'll meet lots of Cubans if you give hitchhikers lifts. It is also easy to arrange a car and driver: this is best organized with a private driver rather than through one of the official cab companies. While few things beat cruising along Havana's Malecón in an old, gas-guzzling Cadillac, a more mundane Lada is a better choice for a long journey.

Money

The only currency worth taking to Cuba is the U.S. dollar. Take as much cash (in small denominations) as you feel comfortable with, and the rest in the form of travelers' checks, which you can exchange for cash in most tourist hotels. Do not take American Express travelers' checks or an Amex charge card, which are not accepted due to the U.S. embargo. Credit cards are accepted by many tourist hotels, restaurants, and shops and can also be used to withdraw cash from a bank. It is quite possible to spend two weeks in Cuba without handling a single peso. You cannot use pesos in tourist establishments, and if you buy anything at a farmer's market or from a street vendor, dollars are equally acceptable. However, most people like to possess some pesos, if only to satisfy a principle. Exchange bureaux called *Cadecas* make it possible to change dollars officially into pesos at the same rate as on the black market.

Souvenirs

Rum and cigars are, of course, the classic souvenirs. While the latter are sold cheaply and illegally on the street, you should buy from official outlets unless you are confident you know a fake Cohiba when you see one. While the Cohiba is the top brand, you may be able to impress cigar aficionados with one of the new brands, such as Cuaba or Trinidad.

Rum comes in many varieties. Havana Club is the best brand. While the three-year-old rum may taste fine in the Cuban sun, it won't when you get home. It is worth paying an extra couple of dollars for the five- or seven-year-old variety. Wash the rum down with some Cubita, the island's home-grown coffee. If you enjoy son or salsa music, make the most of the great range of CDs and cassettes available, and old LPs can be picked up in the street for just a couple of dollars. Cuba will also satisfy anyone's obsession with Che Guevara, whose face emblazons everything from T-shirts to refrigerator magnets. The limited private enterprise permitted since 1993 has seen the blossoming of craftsmanship. There are numerous stalls in and around the Plaza de la Catedral in Old Havana. Trinidad is famous for its lace and embroidery, which is available from street traders.

Accommodation

The best quality accommodation is in Havana and in the beach resorts. Here, many hotels are joint ventures with foreign companies, which know how to please overseas visitors better than their relatively inexperienced Cuban counterparts. Resort accommodation is expensive, with less than four-star accommodation rare in such places. You can find comfortable, atmospheric hotels in Havana with no difficulty. An increasing number of colonial mansions in the old city are being converted into hotels, although most are aimed at the upper end of the market. In provincial cities, the best hotels tend to be impersonal, Soviet-style monstrosities on the edge of town. Small downtown hotels are unlikely to offer more than just basic facilities, and no hot water. Travelers prepared to arrive in Cuba with no accommodation arranged (although immigration officials will give you a hard time if you don't have at least a couple of nights in a hotel pre-booked), should consider staying in a Cuban home. For $10–25 you can rent a room in a private house, and will get a real insight into daily life. Such accommodation was legalized in 1997, but you'll see few signs up. You usually need to just ask around or wait for someone to approach you in the street.

Eating Out

While people would still think you were crazy if you were visiting Cuba for the food, it is easier to get a decent meal now than it was five years ago. As with the hotels, the best food is generally available in Havana and the beach resorts. However, for the tastiest and cheapest meals, you should avoid the state-run restaurants in favor of the *paladares* — the small, family restaurants that were legalized in 1993. While many are very simple, others have printed menus, wine lists, and uniformed staff. Vegetarians are not well catered for. The Cuban diet is thoroughly meat-oriented. Eggs and cheese are easily available in state-run restaurants, but vegans should be prepared to devote time to ensuring a decent diet. The farmers' markets are an excellent source of fruit and vegetables. If you make friends with the staff in your hotel kitchen, they may even cook something especially for you.

Safety

Crime has increased in tandem with the rise in tourism, and it is easy to understand why. Given that the average monthly salary for a Cuban is about $5, as a tourist you will probably be carrying in your pocket the equivalent of at least a year's wages. Most of the Cubans trying to acquire tourists' money do so by selling cigars or themselves, or simply by begging, but some people do resort to petty theft. Physical attacks are extremely rare. Old Havana has the worst reputation for bag-snatchers and pickpockets, and there is a heavy police presence in this area. The streets are not well lit at night, so you should stick to the busier thoroughfares and try to avoid being out late on your own. If you are driving a rental car, try to park it in a guarded parking lot overnight, and pay to have someone keep an eye on it if you leave it for any length of time during the day. Popular ruses are to steal the hubcaps, if not the entire wheel. Insurance for you and your vehicle is a must.

Health

There are few specific health risks in Cuba. The most common problems are sunburn and the odd bout of diarrhea. Vaccinations are recommended against tetanus, typhoid, polio, and also hepatitis A. While there is no malaria in Cuba, there are plenty of mosquitoes, which are particularly troublesome in summer. In 1997, dengue fever was reported in Santiago and parts of southern Cuba. There is no cure for this viral disease, which is carried by mosquitoes, so the best you can do is protect yourself against being bitten. Bring all the medication you think you might need from home. Medicines are available in dollar shops in Havana but are expensive. The drinking water is generally safe. Mineral water is easily available (if expensive) for anyone who prefers to take precautions. Cuba has no poisonous snakes or spiders.

Women Travelers

Men in Cuba enjoy hitting on women, be they Cuban or foreign, but such overtures are almost always good-humored and rarely lead to any kind of harassment. Also, with the system of state-sponsored mass hitchhiking, Cuba is one of the few places in the world where it is safe for women to hitchhike on their own.

ADDRESSES AND CONTACTS

Cuban Interest Section
2630 16th Street, NW
Washington, DC 20009
Tel. (202) 797-8518
Fax (202) 797-8521

Regent Holidays
15 John Street,
Bristol BS1 2HR
Tel. 0117-9211711
(tour operator specializing
in Cuba)

Cuban Embassy
167 High Holborn
London WC1V 6PA
Tel. 071-240 2488.
(tourist office at same address,
tel. 0171-379-1706)

Progressive Tours
12 Porchester Place
London W2 2BS
Tel. 0171-262-1676
(specialist tour operator)

Cuba Solidarity Campaign
c/o Red Rose Club
129 Seven Sisters Road
London N7 7QG
Tel. 0171-263-6452

Journey Latin America
14-16 Devonshire Road,
Chiswick, London W4
2HD
Tel. 0181-747-3108
(Tours and flights)

Center for Cuban Studies
124 W. 23 Street,
New York, NY 10011
Tel. (212) 242-0559

South America Experience
47 Causton Street,
Pimlico, London SW1P
4AT
Tel. 0171-976-5511
(Tours and flights)

Global Exchange, Cuba Project
2017 Mission Street, Ste. 303,
San Francisco, CA 94110
Tel. (415) 255-7296

Marazul Tours
4100 Park Avenue
Weehawken, NJ 07087
Tel. (201) 319-9508
Fax (201) 319-9009
E-mail: marazul@igc.org
(specializes in Cuba
travel)

FURTHER READING

Arenas, R., *Before Night Falls: A Memoir*. New York, 1993.
Baloyra, E.A. & J.A. Morris, *Conflict and Change in Cuba*. New Mexico, 1993.
Barclay, J. *Havana: Portrait of a City*. London, 1993.
Barnet, M., *The Autobiography of a Runaway Slave, Esteban Montejo*. London
Bethell, Leslie, *Cuba: A Short History*. Cambridge, 1993.
Brandon, G., *Santería from Africa to the New World*. Indiana, 1993.
Cabrera Infante, G., *Mea Cuba*. London, 1994.
Calder S. & E. Hatchwell, *Travellers Survival Kit: Cuba*. Oxford, 1996.
Cardoso, E. & A. Helwege, *Cuba After Communism*. Massachussets, 1992.
Castro, F., *Che: A Memoir*. Melbourne, 1994.
Gunn, G., *Cuba in Transition: Options for U.S. Policy*. New York, 1993.
Halperin, M., *Return to Havana: The Decline of Cuban Society under Castro*. Nashville, 1994.
Helly, D., *The Cuban Commission Report: A Hidden History of the Chinese in Cuba (1876)*. Baltimore, 1993.
Liss, S.B., *Fidel! Castro's Political and Social Thought*. Colorado, 1994.
Oppenheimer, A., *Castro's Final Hour*. New York, 1992.
Orozco, R., *Cuba Roja: Cómo viven los cubanos con Fidel Castro*. Madrid, 1993.
Ospina, H.C., *Salsa: Havana Heat, Bronx Beat*. London, 1995.
Pérez, L.A., Jr, *Cuba: Between Reform and Revolution*. New York, 1988.
Pérez Sarduy, P. & J. Stubbs, *Afrocuba*. London, 1993.
Pérez Stable, M., *The Cuban Revolution: Origins, Course and Legacy*. New York, 1993.
Quirk, R.E., *Fidel Castro*. New York, 1993.
Rieff, D., *The Exile: Cuba in the Heart of Miami*. London, 1994.
Smith, S., *Land of Miracles*. London, 1996.
Szulc, T., *Fidel: A Critical Portrait*. London, 1989.
Timerman, J., *Cuba: A Journey*. London, 1994.
Williams, S., *Cuba: The Land, the Culture, the History, the People*. London, 1994.

FICTION

Cabrera Infante, G., *View of Dawn in the Tropics*. London, 1990.
Carpentier, A., *Explosion in a Cathedral*. London, 1971.
García, C., *Dreaming in Cuban*. New York, 1992.
Greene, G., *Our Man in Havana*. London, 1994.
Hemingway, E., *The Old Man and the Sea*. London, 1994.
Iyer, P. *Cuba and the Night*. London, 1995.

FACTS AND FIGURES

GEOGRAPHY

Official name: República de Cuba.

Situation: Cuba lies in the Caribbean Sea, between 19 49' and 23 18' N and 74 8' and 84 57' W; it is the largest of the Greater Antilles, extending 775 miles in length, 118 miles at its widest point, 19 miles at its narrowest.

Surface area: 44,218 sq. miles (UK 94,570 sq. miles).

Administrative division: 14 *provincias,* divided into 169 *municipios.*

Capital: Ciudad de la Habana (Havana), population 2,100,000 (1989 estimate).

Other large towns (population 1989 estimate x 1,000): Santiago de Cuba (405), Camagüey (283), Holguín (228), Guantánamo (200), Santa Clara (194) and Cienfuegos (123).

Infrastructure (1995 figures): 9,376 miles paved roads, 20,735 miles unpaved. Paved roads are poorly maintained but the relatively small volume of traffic means wear and tear are minimal. The most important roads are the Ocho Vías, an eight-lane highway that runs west from Havana to Pinar del Río and eastward to Camagüey (incomplete), and the older Carretera Central (709 miles), which crosses the entire country from Pinar del Río to Santiago and runs through the middle of many towns and cities; the Vía Blanca connects Havana and Varadero. Cuba has 9,002 miles of railtrack; 5, 982 miles of this is used by the sugar industry, the rest being run for public service by *Ferrocarriles de Cuba.* The main international airports are Havana, Varadero, Santiago, Camagüey, and Holguín; the state airline, *Cubana de Aviación,* operates international and domestic flights. The main ports are Havana, Santiago, Cienfuegos and Matanzas.

Relief and landscape: wide and fertile plains predominate in Cuba (60% of which is under 650 feet above sea level); about a third of the island is mountainous; the principal range is the Sierra Maestra, which extends 150 miles in the southeastern corner of the island; its tallest peak is Pico Turquino (6,501 feet); the highest point in the Escambray mountains north of Trinidad is Pico San Juan (3,465 feet); the Cordillera de Guaniguanico in Pinar del Río province includes the Sierra de los Organos, with its famous *mogotes,* large limestone humps that rise dramatically out of the flat tobacco fields of the Viñales valley and conceal caves and subterranean rivers; Cuba has more than 200 rivers, but most are short and shallow, average length 25 miles; the longest is Río Cauto, which extends for 230 miles along the northern edge of the Sierra Maestra, although the best waterfalls are along Río Hanabanilla in central Cuba; the south coast is scattered with marshes, the largest being the protected Ciénaga de Zapata in Matanzas province, and dense mangrove forest can be found in places; by contrast, the northern coast is mostly rocky, except for the central part which has some of the island's finest white sand beaches, most famously at

Varadero near Havana and Santa Lucía near Camagüey; Cuba is surrounded by more than 1,600 tiny islands and keys; Isla de la Juventud is the largest (900 sq. miles); coral reefs skirt the main island, the longest stretching for some 250 miles along the north coast of Camagüey province; the water is very clear and perfect for diving.

Temperature and rainfall: Cuba has a tropical climate, with a rainy season from May to October and a dry season from November to April; the temperatures are cooler during the dry season, but there is always plenty of sun; temperatures across the island vary very little, ranging from around 61°F in January to near 90°F in August, but as a rule hover closer to the annual average of 77°F; increased humidity in the summer brings the main difference. North-easterly trade winds temper the heat in all but the extreme summer months of July and August, which are sultry and particularly unpleasant in Havana. The average annual rainfall is 61 inches. Torrential rainstorms are possible at any time, but mostly in summer and autumn. Oriente tends to receive less rain than the west.

Hurricanes: from September to November, Cuba is vulnerable to hurricanes, when winds can reach over 150 m.p.h. and bring torrential rain; like many Caribbean islands, Cuba has suffered devastation by hurricanes; more than 4,000 people died in Hurricane Flora in 1963; better advance warning means that subsequent storms have brought lower death tolls but warnings cannot prevent crop devastation; the so-called Storm of the Century in 1993 killed about 200 people and flattened crops, doing millions of dollars worth of damage.

Flora and fauna: Cuba has about 8,000 species of plant and small, isolated pockets of tropical rainforest in the Sierra Maestra and Escambray mountains; about a quarter of the island's surface is wooded, but only a fraction of the species (including cedar and mahogany) used abundantly by colonial furniture-makers survive; on the other hand, Cuba has an estimated 70 million palm trees, among the highest such concentrations in the world; the elegant royal palm, with its smooth, silvery trunk, is seen everywhere from sugar plantations to courtyards in the center of Havana; Cuba has about 300 species of birds (7% endemic), including parrots, the Cuban trogon, which has red, white, and blue plumage — the colors of the Cuban flag — and is the national bird, and the bee hummingbird, the smallest in the world; Cuba has no poisonous snakes and few large mammals living in the wild, though wild boar and deer are found in the Guana-hacabibes peninsula in Pinar del Río province, and monkeys live in some isolated areas; the protected swamps of the Ciénaga de Zapata are home to crocodiles.

POPULATION

Population (1997): 11,000,000 (1970: 8.5 million).

Annual population growth: 1970-1980: 1.3%; 1980-1990: 0.9%; 1990-1995 0.9%; projected population in 2000 is 11.5 million.

Population density (1992): 251 inhabitants per sq. mile.

Urbanization (1992): 75% (1970: 60.2%).

Fertility: a Cuban woman has an average of 1.54 children (1997).

Age structure: one in three Cubans is under 26.

Birthrate (1997): 13.21 per 1,000.

Mortality rate (1997): 7.42 per 1,000.

Infant mortality (1997): 7.1 per 1,000 live births (1960: 65 per 1,000).

Average life expectancy (1997): 76 years.

Average household (1981

census): 4 persons.
Doctors (1992): 1 doctor per
231 inhabitants.
*Daily per capita calorie
consumption (1993):* 1,780
(compared with 2,845 in
1989 and the UN recom-
mended level of 3,000).
Literacy (1992): 95%.
Education (1989): 95%
enrolled at primary school;
89% at secondary school;
17.2% at tertiary level.
Universities (1989): there are
40 universities; enrolment
2,304 students per 100,000
inhabitants.
*Social Development Index,
UNDP Human Development
Index (1994):* 89th position
(in "medium human develop-

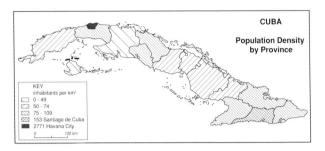

ment" category); UK 10th,
U.S. 8th positions; total 173
positions.
Ethnic composition: officially
66% Hispanic, 12% black,
21.9% mulatto (mixed
Hispanic and black), and
0.1% Asian.
Languages: Spanish, with
regional variations affecting

both accent and vocabulary;
African words restricted
mainly to religious terms.
Religion: there is no
established church. Some
Cubans are Roman Catholic,
there are many Protestant
churches, and Afro-Cuban
religions (Santería) are very
popular.

ECONOMY

*(Since 1989 and the onset of Cuba's economic crisis, data on the economy has been largely
unavailable. Cuban economic statistics do not feature in the reports of international financial
institutions such as the IMF. This means that only a partial picture of the country's economy is
possible.)*

Currency unit: peso (Ps).
GDP (1993): Ps10bn.
Per capita GDP (1993):
Ps917.
*Economic growth (real GDP
growth):* 0.1% (1989); -3.1%
(1990); -25% (1991); -18%
(1992); -13.3% (1993); 0.7%
(1994); 2.5% (1995); 7.8%
(1996); 2.5% (1997).
Foreign debt (1997):
US$11bn.
*Structure of the economy
(1989): share of GDP:*
industry (46%); commerce
(20.1%); agriculture (15.9%);
construction (9.3%). 1996:
industry (31%); agriculture

(7%); services (62%).
*Working population by
sector:* services 47.7%;
industry 28.5%; agriculture
23.8%.
Budget deficit (1993):
Ps5.2bn.
Exports: (1996) US$2.1bn;
(1994) US$1.7bn (1989
US$5.4bn).
Imports: (1996) US$3.5bn;
(1994) US$2.5bn (1989
US$1.3bn).
*Main exports and services by
value (1993):*
sugar (US$720m), tourism
(US$650m), nickel (US$157m),
seafood (US$100m), tobacco

(US$50m).
*Main imports by value
(1988):* machinery and
transport equipment
(Ps2,410m), food, beverages,
and tobacco (Ps730m),
chemicals (Ps434m).
Principal trading partners:
percentage of exports to
Europe fell from 83% in
1990 to 67% in 1993, while
those to the Americas rose
from 7% in 1990 to 14% in
1993. Latin America
supplied 47% of Cuban
imports in 1993 compared
with 7% in 1990; those from
Europe fell from 87% to

36%. Main trading partners (exports): Canada, Portugal, Netherlands, Japan, Spain; (imports): Spain, France, Canada, Italy, UK, Mexico, Japan, and Canada.
Joint ventures: by 1993 it was estimated that US$500 million had been invested in joint ventures; about a quarter in tourism. More than 410 (1993) commercial firms are backed by foreign capital.
Trade relations with North America: Under the terms of the U.S. economic embargo, no U.S. companies or agencies are permitted to trade with Cuba. Canada imported approximately US$120 million of goods from Cuba in 1994; its exports that year totaled approximately US$70 million.
Trade relations with Britain: In 1993 the value of UK exports to Cuba was £14

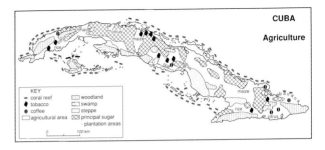

CUBA
Agriculture

KEY
coral reef | woodland
tobacco | swamp
coffee | steppe
agricultural area | principal sugar plantation areas
0 ___ 100 km

million, a fall of 50% on the 1992 figure. In 1994, however, British exports rose by 80%, comprising mostly cereals. In 1994, Cuban exports to Britain averaged US$1.3 million per month, consisting mostly of agricultural and sugar products.
Aid and development relations with North America: The U.S. does not give any bilateral aid to Cuba and uses its influence in international financial institutions to prevent economic support going

there. U.S. NGOs and church groups raise money and support projects in Cuba. The Canadian government gives some development aid to Cuba.
Aid and development relations with Britain: Official British aid to Cuba is negligible or non-existent. A number of British development agencies have projects in Cuba, and the Cuba Solidarity Campaign organizes volunteers to go and work in the country.

HISTORY AND POLITICS

Key historical dates: * c. 1000BC: Siboneys settle in Cuba, followed later by Taínos from Orinoco basin * 1492: Columbus sights Cuba and lands at Gibara on 28 October * 1511-14: Diego Velásquez and Pánfilo Narváez oversee the occupation of Cuba and the foundation of the colony's first towns * 1607: Havana replaces Santiago de Cuba as capital * 1762: the British

occupy Havana for 10 months and break Spain's monopoly on trade * 1789: a royal decree authorizes free trade in slaves * 1812: the Aponte uprising, the first major rebellion by slaves in Cuba * 1818: Spain opens Cuban ports to free international trade * 1837: the laying of Cuba's first railway (the first in Latin America) * 1848-51: Narciso López, former soldier in

Spanish army, leads three failed invasions of Cuba, with aim of annexing the island to the U.S. * 1868-78: the Ten Years' War in Oriente province fails to free Cuba of Spanish rule * 1878: in the "Protest of Baraguá," Antonio Maceo denounces the Pact of Zanjón which ended the war and leaves the country * 1886: Spain abolishes slavery * 1892: José Martí founds the Cuban Revolutionary Party in Florida * 1895: the Cuban war of independence begins on February 24 * 1898: the U.S. intervenes following the sinking of the *USS Maine* and in December signs the Treaty of Paris with Spain * May 5, 1902: Cuba is declared a Republic and U.S. forces withdraw * 1903: Cuba adopts the Platt Amendment, allowing the Americans to intervene to "defend" Cuban independence and granting them a naval base at Guantánamo * 1924: Gerardo Machado elected president, beginning of a harsh dictatorship * 1933: a general strike forces Machado out, and rebel sergeants under Fulgencio Batista take over * 1940: Batista wins the presidency but loses it four years later * 1952: Batista stages a coup, "abolishes" the constitution, and presides over ruthless military dictatorship * July 26, 1953: Fidel Castro leads an attack on the Moncada barracks in Santiago * May 1955: Fidel Castro is released and leaves for Mexico * 1956: Castro and 81 revolutionaries return to Cuba aboard the *Granma* yacht and launch guerrilla insurgency from the Sierra Maestra mountains * Jan. 1, 1959: Fulgencio Batista flees Havana and the army surrenders * 1959: Castro's new government introduces agrarian reform and other radical changes * 1960: American assets are nationalized and Washington imposes trade embargo * April 1961: the Bay of Pigs invasion by U.S.-backed Cuban exiles fails * October 1962: the Cuban Missile Crisis * 1965: Cuba's alliance of revolutionary parties reorganized as the Partido Comunista de Cuba (PCC) * 1967: Che Guevara killed in Bolivia * 1968: a "revolutionary offensive" includes the nationalization of all remaining small businesses * 1970: the attempt to produce a 10-million ton sugar harvest fails, prompting closer links with the USSR to avert economic crisis * 1975: first PCC congress convened * 1976: new constitution and assemblies of People's Power approved * 1977: Washington and Havana re-establish limited diplomatic relations * 1978: Cuban exiles in Miami are allowed to return to Cuba for family visits * 1980: the Mariel boatlift results in the emigration of 125,000 Cubans to Miami * 1986: the Rectification of Errors ends brief experiment with private enterprise * 1988: an accord in New York brings the withdrawal of Cuban troops from Angola * 1989: trial and execution of General Ochoa * 1990: the "Special Period in Peace Time" introduces massive austerity measures to Cuba * 1991: 4th PCC Congress decides to admit Catholics into the party for the first time * 1992: Torricelli Bill, tightening up the U.S. trade embargo, passed in Washington * 1993: depenalization of the dollar and introduction of limited private enterprise * Aug. 8, 1994: riot in Havana sparks the biggest exodus of boatpeople since Mariel; private farmers' markets are legalized. 1995: Cuba and the U.S. agree over increase of immigrant visas granted to Cubans wishing to leave the country * 1996: Helms-Burton Bill is finally passed, in watered-down form, following the shooting down by Cuba of two aircraft flown by Brothers to the Rescue * 1997: the remains of Che Guevara are returned to Cuba from Bolivia and interred amid great ceremony in a mausoleum in Santa Clara * 1998: Pope John Paul II makes a five-day visit and criticises both the U.S. embargo and Cuba's imprisonment of political prisoners; the fifth Communist Party Congress vows to maintain Cuba's socialist framework.

Constitution: Cuba's socialist constitution states that "all the power belongs to the working people and is exercised through the Assemblies of People's Power." The *Asamblea Nacional de Poder Popular*, with 589 members (1997), is

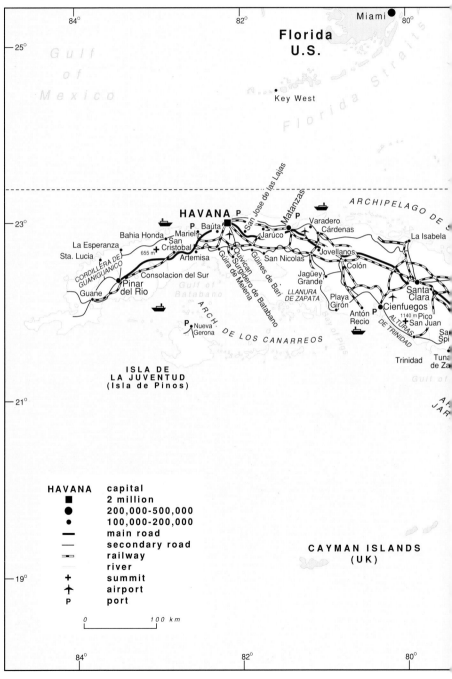

Miami

**Florida
U.S.**

84°   82°   80°
25°

Gulf

of

Mexico

Key West

Florida Straits

ARCHIPELAGO DE

23°   **HAVANA** P
P Baúta   San Jose de las Lajas   Matanzas P
Bahia Honda Mariel   Jarúco   Varadero   La Isabela
La Esperanza   San   Cárdenas
Sta. Lucia   Cristobal   655 m   Quivican   San Nicolas   Jovellanos
CORDILLERA DE   Artemisa   Güira de Melena   Güines de Barí   Colón
GUANIGUANICO   Surgidero de Batabano   Jagüey   Santa
Consolacion del Sur   Grande   LLANURA   Clara
Pinar   Gulf of   DE ZAPATA   Playa   Cienfuegos
Guane   del Rio   Batabano   Girón   Antón   1140 m Pico   Sa
Recio P   San Juan   Spi
P   Nueva   ARCH.   ALTURAS DE TRINIDAD
Gerona   DE LOS CANARREOS   Bay of Pigs   Trinidad   Tuna
de Za

21°   ISLA DE   Gulf of
LA JUVENTUD
(Isla de Pinos)   A
JAR

HAVANA   capital
■   2 million
●   200,000-500,000
•   100,000-200,000
—   main road
—   secondary road   **CAYMAN ISLANDS**
≔   railway   **(UK)**
river
19°   ✚   summit
✈   airport
P   port

0   100 km

84°   82°   80°

elected by the people every five years. The 30-member *Consejo de Estado* and the 44-member *Consejo de Ministros* are the two highest government bodies. *Head of State:* Fidel Castro Ruz, constitutional head of state since December 2, 1976, although de facto leader since 1959. Titles: President of the Council of State and Council of Ministers, Secretary-General of the Communist Party, and Commander-in-Chief of the Revolutionary Armed Forces.

Political Parties: Partido Comunista de Cuba (PCC), the "supreme leading force of society and state," is the only legal political party. *Armed forces (1991 Western estimates):* army 145,000 (including conscripts), navy 13,500, airforce 22,000; army reserves 135,000; State Security troops 120,000; border guards 4,000, EJT (youth army) 100,000; people's militia 1.3 million.

Membership of international organizations: UN and UN organizations; Caribbean Tourism Association; Caribbean Trade Organization; Association of Caribbean States.

Media and communications: 343 radios, 203 television sets, and 56.4 telephones per 1,000 inhabitants (UK/U.S.: 1,146/2,123 radios, 435/815 television sets, 477/789 telephones). Newspapers (these figures are based on the late 1980s, since then shortages have drastically reduced newspaper output): since 1990 *Granma* (400,000 circulation; Cuban Communist Party) has been the only daily newspaper available; *Juventud Rebelde* (250,000; Unión de Jovenes Comunistas) and *Trabajadores* (150,000; CTC) are now only weekly; an international edition of *Granma* also appears weekly, in English, French, Spanish, and Portuguese; 15 provincial papers appear weekly if at all. One of the most widely-read monthly journals is the cultural magazine, *Bohemia.* Cuba has 5 national radio stations and one international network (Radio Habana Cuba), in addition to about 50 local stations. There are two national television networks, Cubavisión and Tele-Rebelde, which broadcast only in the evenings except on Sundays.

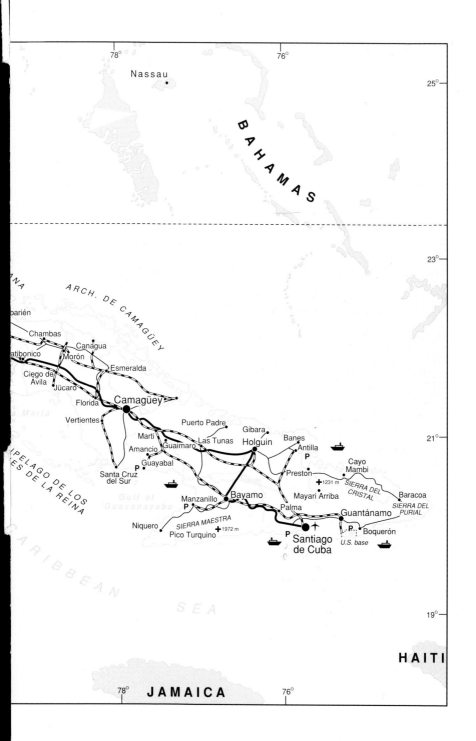